THE OFFICIAL
GOURMET
H·A·N·D·B·O·O·K

PASQUALE
BRUNO, JR.

Contemporary Books, Inc.
Chicago

Library of Congress Cataloging in Publication Data

Bruno, Pasquale.
The official gourmet handbook.

1. Gastronomy—Anecdotes, facetiae, satire, etc.
I. Title.
PN6231.G35B78 1984 641.01'30207 84-4295
ISBN 0-8092-5475-1

Published by Contemporary Books, Inc.
180 North Michigan Avenue, Chicago, Illinois 60601
Manufactured in the United States of America
Library of Congress Catalog Card Number: 84-4295
International Standard Book Number: 0-8092-5475-1

Published simultaneously in Canada by Beaverbooks, Ltd.
195 Allstate Parkway, Valleywood Business Park
Markham, Ontario L3R 4T8 Canada

I pray that death may strike me
in the middle of a large meal.
I wish to be buried under the tablecloth
Between four large dishes.
And I desire that this short inscription
Should be engraved on my tombstone:
Here lies the first poet
Ever to die of indigestion.

Marc-Antoine Desaugiers

PART I

THE GOURMET WORLD

PART II

HOW TO EAT OUT

CONTENTS

PART III

ENTERTAINING CHEZ VOUS

APPENDIX A

APPENDIX B

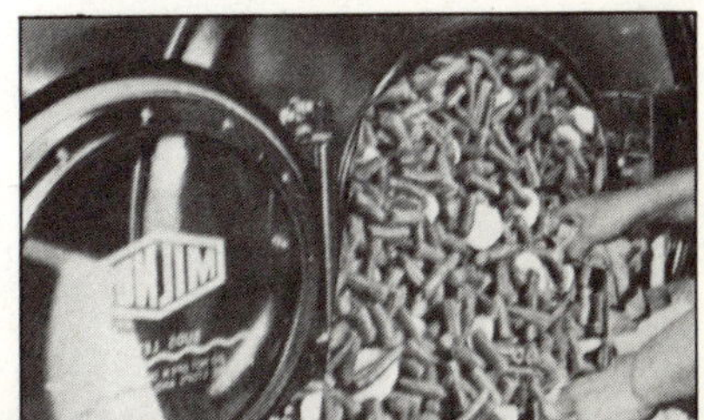

Does not this art in fact embrace all branches of human activity? Is not the art of feeding oneself one of the primordial needs of man?
Brillat-Savarin
The Physiology of Taste (1825)

INTRODUCTION

Most of us, on one occasion or another, have had to face an embarrassing situation connected with entertaining at home, dining out, ordering wine, tipping, or other matters concerning food and drink. Many of us have been humiliated, unnerved, sat upon, jostled, and made to feel just plain miserable in restaurants and at parties—all because of sheer ignorance of the situations and how best to handle them.

It doesn't matter what you *think* you are—be it a discerning gourmet, a nondiscerning gourmet, a journeyman gourmet, or a would-be gourmet. You need this book to help you make your way through the complex world of Gourmania. If, on the other hand, you stuff food into your mouth for the sole purpose of getting an oral fix, this book is not meant for you. But then again, don't we all aspire in some way to be a gourmet?

Let me give an example to illustrate why you should read this book. I have a friend who refuses to eat in a public place or entertain or cook for anyone. Just prior to adopting this isolationism his inner problems were openly manifested (it was just a matter of time): his hands would shake on lifting a menu; he would stutter when ordering a bacon, lettuce, and tomato sandwich; he would sometimes break into a cold sweat when passing a fancy restaurant. Why? Because he had been ridiculed and embarrassed in restaurants, cafeterias, coffee shops, snack bars, and even fast-food drive-throughs.

Once, on a plane trip to Florida, the flight crew hijacked *him.* They locked him in the rest room for the entire flight. Why? Because he couldn't decide between the Chicken Kiev and the Beef Stroganoff. Passengers started to shout, "Throw him out, throw him out." The captain had him brought to the flight deck to be reprimanded. As he walked back to his seat people tried to trip him; a little girl squirted a packet of salad dressing on his shirt. Another time, a coffee shop owner chased him with a knife when he asked, "What is a francheezie?"

He once gave a dinner party for friends at his apartment. Trying to serve Duck à l'Orange at a sit-down dinner for twenty people in a studio apartment is sort of like having a Polish wedding reception in a Winnebago: disaster lurks everywhere. To this day, of the twenty who were there, eighteen refuse to talk to him (some have sent threatening letters), one is in a home, and his best friend, a lawyer, has filed a class action suit.

The capper that put him into kitchen isolation came when he ordered a red wine to accompany Dover sole. ("I like red wine," he later told me.) All the people in the restaurant got up and left, the waiter blew out the candle on his table, his date left with one of the busboys, and the restaurant lights were turned out. Sitting there in the dark, he thought to himself, "Enough is enough." Since then he has refused to eat outside of his kitchen or to see anyone.

Several months ago I sent my friend a copy of this book. His psychiatrist tells me it is doing wonders for him. Recently he talked about the possibility of ordering out for pizza. That's progress.

PART I
THE GOURMET WORLD

JEAN ANTHELME BRILLAT-SAVARIN
(1755–1826)

Tell me what you eat, and I will tell you what you are.

Brillat-Savarin
The Physiology of Taste (1825)

1

IDENTIFYING THE REAL GOURMET

In the complex world of *haute cuisine*, you must have an identity.

Gourmand: A person who has a tendency to indulge in food and drink to excess (where more might not be enough).

Gourmet: A person who is a first-rate judge of food and drink and can appreciate quality and flavor with discriminating taste (where less is probably better).

Epicure: A person whose taste is highly refined and who takes great pleasure in foods and drinks. (Less should not only be better; it must be great.)

Glutton: A person who is a greedy and voracious eater and drinker. Some circles would classify this person as being uncivilized. (Nothing matters here except quantity—a disciple of the Shovel-It-In School of Dining.)

Gastronome: A person who is an expert in all aspects of the art and science of good eating (a critic of all of the above).

If you still have an identity problem, consider this definition from *Webster's:*

Gourmandise: "The tastes or connoisseurship of a gourmand."

Now, to put the frosting on the cake, so to speak, consider this comment (and others throughout the book) from Brillat-Savarin, the great French gastronome:

● ●

> *Those who interpret gourmandise have forgotten the social gourmandise which combines the elegance of Athens, the luxury of Rome, and the delicacy of France. Such gourmandise orders with discernment, supervises with wisdom, savors with enthusiasm, judges with profundity. It is a precious attribute which may well be esteemed a virtue, for it is the source of our purest delights.*

● ●

Brillat-Savarin extends the definition to say that "gourmandise is the enemy of excess—every man who gives himself indigestion or gets drunk runs the risk of no longer being a true gourmand."

Brillat-Savarin's pronouncements do tighten up the wrinkles somewhat for serious eaters, food critics, those prone to gout, and second-helpers as well. Gourmet Emptor!

O ye Gods, what pleasure I have denied myself up to now by being over-fastidious in my tastes.

Artaxerxes
King of Persia

2

FAMOUS FOOD PEOPLE

Here are brief profiles of some of the famous, and infamous, individuals in the world of cookery and cuisine—past and present. Learn them well; they are names that are frequently dropped when food people get together to gnaw and jaw.

Brillat-Savarin, Jean Anthelme (1755–1826). Politician, gastronome, lawyer. Author of *Physiologie du Goût*, a gastronomical work that is a compendium of the art of living. Little-known fact: he spent three years in America as a refugee and played in the orchestra in a New York theater.

Escoffier, Auguste (1847–1935). Chef, restaurateur, author. Emperor William II said to him, "I am the emperor of Germany, but you are the emperor of chefs." His best-known works are *Le Guide Culinaire* and *Ma Cuisine*. Little-known fact: invented the dish Peach

Melba, named after the Australian singer, Nellie Melba.

Longworth, General Dewey (1910–1975). Food service expert, bulletin writer, author. Invented the mess hall concept for the armed services. Author of 244 bulletins that outline the proper methods for feeding troops in large numbers. Little-known fact: while a prisoner of the Japanese during World War II he learned all about rice. In 1951 he authored a book about the dangers of rice called *Against the Grain.*

Tallevent (1326–1395). Cook, author of one of the oldest books on cookery, *Viandier.*

La Varenne (1630–1700). A great chef. Author of the first systematically planned books on cookery, including *Le Cuisinier Français,* published about 1651. Little-known fact: carried love notes between Henry IV and his mistress.

Kolmar, Adafi (1921–1968). Born of Hungarian and Egyptian parents, Adafi became famous for his uncanny ability to use herbs and spices as a main meal. His Fried Paprika-Peppercorns Kabob, and Mock Marjoram Chicken are legendary. Little-known fact: worked for a time as a chef for Charles DeGaulle.

Careme, Marie-Antonin (1784–1833). Cook, author. Known as the cook of kings and the king of cooks. He toiled for Talleyrand, King George IV, Czar Alexander, Baron de Rothschild. His most famous work was *Le Pattissier Royal Parisien.* Little-known fact: he was frequently offered big money by many heads of state, by food companies for television endorsements, and by Charles DeGaulle to become his chef. He refused all such offers and died poor.

Talleyrand, Charles Maurice (1754–1838). Diplomat, statesman, gastronome. He was sadly lacking in moral scruples but set a table that was pure gastronomical showmanship. He believed that the food and drink that he offered his guests played an important part in helping him maintain his lofty position. Little-known fact: He was an abbot and later a bishop, and much later he was excommunicated. Was said to be the first chef used by Charles DeGaulle, but this is in doubt.

Freiburg, Abby (1927-). Author, cooking school teacher, writer. Ms. Freiburg has stumped long and hard to elevate the role of "woman as chef." She has filed lawsuits against many of today's great chefs for piracy of her recipes. She once had an affair with the now great chef and restaurateur, Paul Troisalain. Ms. Freiburg maintains that during this affair Mr. Troisalain hypnotized her into revealing all of her cooking secrets and that he stole her rough drawings of what later became the food processor. She flunked a tryout to become a chef for Charles DeGaulle.

Curnosky, Maurice Edmond Sailland (1872–1956). Author. Prince of gastronomes. His love of food was legendary. He wrote of food and life and founded the Academy of Gastronomes, an illustrious society of serious eaters.

Marengo, Willy (1784–1845). Cook, author, gourmet. Willy invented several dishes that are, to this day, the backbone of classic cuisine—Shrimp de Jonghe, Fritto Misto, Range-top Stuffing. Many have tried to connect Willy with the dishes Veal Marengo and Chicken Marengo. Willy decried this connection (he did have a brother whose nickname was Chicken, however) and took great offense at being associated with food of that sort. Willy spent the last nine years of his life as a restaurant critic for the illustrious magazine *Cochons Tout le Monde*. He refused a job as chef for Charles DeGaulle.

Gourmets Gallery

On the next few pages are candid shots of some of the Real Gourmets of today. By the time you finish this book you, too, could be on your way to a spot in this Gourmets Gallery.

Murray Klein, the *éminence grise* behind Zabar's, the great food emporium in New York City, catering a party for the Royals. (That's Murray on the right with the tray.)

Pierre Franey—surely of gastronome stature—is shown working at the piano—and cooking up a medley of fine cookies and desserts.

Beloved by all Real Gourmets, **James Beard** is shown coming out of a bookstore where he just finished pushing his newest book, *Beard on Ducks*. Mr. Beard is clearly a gastronome, having passed his epicure test many years ago.

An early picture of **Abby Freiburg Mandel,** whom we all know today as the "food processor queen." Abby is shown—pre-food processor days—working the dough for *chrust,* a Polish sugared biscuit. In the background her assistants are twisting the dough to form these delectable treats. Needless to say, Abby now uses a food processor to make all of her biscuits.

The darling of the gourmet set, **Craig Claiborne,** is caught in one of his more embarrassing moments. While serving as an apprentice at the renowned three-star restaurant La Pyramide, in Vienne, France, Craig used plastic roses in a table setting. Here Madame Point, the owner, is chastising Craig for this *faux pas.*

A

Jacques Pepin, the ubiquitous gourmet and cooking school teacher, is shown on the road. Jacques, in photo A, is giving a private cooking lesson to the wives of wealthy Japanese industrialists in Osaka. In photo B, Jacques has just finished preparing the great Scottish dish Haggis, a sheep's stomach stuffed with a pudding made of sheep's innards and oatmeal, and is being led triumphantly out of the cooking class, accompanied by bagpipers and bottle clashers.

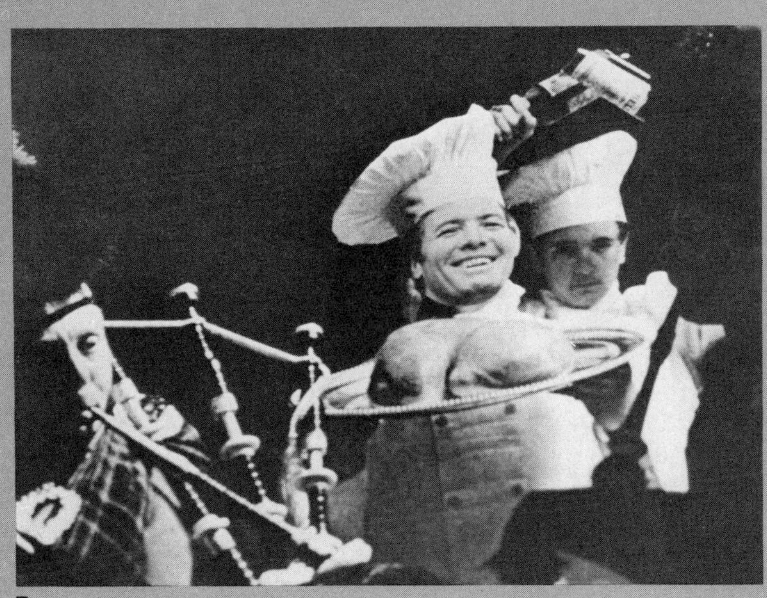

B

It should go without saying, but I'll say it anyway: men dancing together is *not* permitted in a Real Gourmet restaurant. In fact, men who have tried this have been banned into restaurant oblivion. These two men—**Buffo Carbone** and **Phil "Daddy Longlegs" Zanzarone**—were within a notch of becoming Real Gourmets, when they pulled this little *capriola* at a posh restaurant in Sicily. Now they are *persona non benvenuto* in every gourmet restaurant in Italy.

Simone Beck. Along with Mesdames Bertholle and Child, Simone authored Volume One of *Mastering the Art of French Cooking,* and, with Julia, Volume Two—two cookbooks that you will find in the kitchen of every Real Gourmet. A no-nonsense cook, Simone believes in *fresh,* going right to the source for her foodstuffs. Here she is shown shopping for chickens and rabbits in a French market. Simone is, of course, at the gastronome level in the culinary pecking order. In fact, her apron, shopping basket (left arm), and taste buds (not shown) will become part of the Culinary Hall of Fame, located at Mougins (Alpes-Maritimes).

Carl Sontheimer, the man who started the culinary revolution in America, the sire of the food processor, the gourmet's guru. Carl is shown working in his "secret" test kitchen buried deep somewhere in Long Island Sound off Greenwich, Connecticut. It is rumored that Mr. Sontheimer is working on a highly classified product that, according to a well-respected source, will launch Phase II of the "Gourmet Revolution." Speculation has it that it has something to do with a truffle-making machine or cultivation of truffles underwater. The gourmet world is watching the waters off Greenwich Point in anticipation of something big. Mr.Sontheimer has informed *The Official Gourmet Handbook* that the Processor Gigantica shown in Appendix B is a "technical disaster" and that "It will never sell."

Paul Bocuse, owner of the famous three-star restaurant Paul Bocuse, in Collognes-au-Mont-d'Or (a suburb of Lyon), has been called "the world's greatest living chef." That honor is under protest by several other living chefs, who are also laying claim to the title. Bocuse's cooking feats are on a grand scale: "I know how to prepare chicken 146 different ways; and, from a dozen eggs, I can create 36 distinctive meals," he says proudly. Bocuse does not confine his culinary talents to France. He has a restaurant in Tokyo and a cooking school in Osaka, and there is rumor that he has his eye on a place for a restaurant in Peking. "Just think of what I could do with all those ducks," he said with a gleam in his eye. Japan recently honored Bocuse by striking a medal in his honor; it is available for purchase at all Bocuse restaurants, cooking schools, and your neighborhood K-Mart.

Julia Child. What more needs to be said? A household name that is always on the lips of the Real Gourmet: "Julia said . . ." "Julia does it this way." "Julia uses . . ." On and on it goes *ad cook and stirum.* Julia Child has been the "mother in the kitchen" to a whole generation of aspiring gourmets. "Julia saved my marriage," said Blanch Bland, a housewife from Topeka, Kansas. "She inspired me to go beyond meat loaf, casseroles, and pot roast to poulet, poisson, pêche, and pomme de terre." "My husband had told me, 'Either you learn how to cook real gourmet food, or I'll find someone who can.' So I switched from watching the soaps to watching Julia. In no time I became a Real Gourmet cook." And the beat goes on. Always one step ahead of emerging cuisines, Julia has moved into Yugoslav cooking—"the cuisine phenomenon of the late '80s," says Julia. Ms. Child is pictured here (in native Yugoslav dress) presenting one of the Slav dishes that will be featured on her new television series, "Julia in Dubrovnik."

Joel Dean and Giorgio DeLuca, owners of the famous New York food emporium Dean & DeLuca, are shown in a warehouse in the Moluccas selecting garlic for their store.

"Twice a year we retrace the routes of Marco Polo and Vasco da Gama in search of gourmet foodstuffs for our customers," say the peripatetic pair. True gourmets to the core, Dean & DeLuca have introduced a bushel basketful of new gourmet foods to the all-consuming gourmet groupies that abound in New York City. "Many of our customers wait at the docks for our ships to come in to see what new foods we have discovered," says Joel Dean. "Most often we have a sellout on a product before it leaves the dock," he adds exultantly. Some of the more exciting gourmet foods that Dean & DeLuca have introduced to the New World are Niña, Pinta, and Santa Maria beans, sun-dried oysters, acorn oil, cottage cheese in a tube, *ravioli rabarbaro* (rhubarb ravioli), and *pâté de popcorn.* Giorgio, an olive oil aficionado, is studying the possibility of an underwater pipeline—*condotto di olio*—between northern Italy and New York City, to assure a steady and fresh supply of olive oil to his store. *Buona fortuna,* Giorgio.

Once fire was discovered, the instinct for improvement made men bring food to it, in the first place to dry it, and afterwards to put on the fire to cook.

Brillat-Savarin
The Physiology of Taste (1825)

3

CUISINE DEFINED

Cooking is an ancient art, given birth when man first discovered that meat thrown into a fire came out tastier and easier to eat. To be a Real Gourmet you need not understand the cooking habits of Ancient Greece, Rome, or other early civilizations; be aware of the fact, however, that all cooking techniques and many dishes that we know today are direct descendants of Greek and Italian cooking.

In the centuries that followed those ancient times, up to the present, and into the future, dishes were, are being, and will continue to be changed and refined. Recipes are altered, stolen, changed, passed around, and changed again.

New foods were introduced to the New World: tomatoes, rice, potatoes, beans. Advancing technology gave us even more food for thought: canned foods, frozen foods, artificial foods, processed foods (some with an expiration date clear into the 21st century), tube cheese, boil-in-a-bag foods, Stove-Top stuffing, mock truffles, frozen dinners on a stick, and so forth.

In a never-ending quest to please the fickle taste buds of the people, food companies and restaurants are putting together combinations of foods that make the mouths of the Real Gourmets dry up like barren oil fields.

It is not enough, anymore, to classify food and restaurants by nationality alone—French, Italian, Mexican, German, etc. More and more, foods of countries, regions, states, and ethnic groups (and ethnic groups within ethnic groups), are being mixed and mashed together. It takes fast feet, a fast shopping cart, and careful reading of every cookbook, food magazine, and restaurant guide to stay on top of the waves in the heavy seas of cooking.

The Official Gourmet Handbook's crack research team, headed by Dr. Wilma Felcher, has compiled a list of food classifications—the first one ever attempted. This is the most definitive and up-to-date listing ever assembled. Thousands of chefs, food writers, short-order cooks, noted restaurateurs, street vendors, dishwashers, and rest room attendants were surveyed. The final results were cross-checked, double-checked, hat-checked, body-checked, and chubby-checked.

A NEW CUISINE IS BORN

Here, then, is the Dr. Wilma Felcher record of types of cuisine.* To allow quick reference the types are classified by popularity and acceptance among Real Gourmets: *out, in,* and *coming.*

Out	*In*	*Coming*
Cuisine Minceur	Cal-Cal	Cuisine Bourgeois
Nouvelle Cuisine	Cal-Kan	Metro-Pole
Nouveau Italiano	Al-Po	Thai-Juan
Nouvelle Rochelle	Haut-Tex	Nouveau York
Nouvelle Jersey	Chin-Chin	Cuisine Complicato
Nouvelle Deal	Swiss-Miss	Cuisine Vetisse
Nouvelle Fangled	Chi-Chi	Cuisine Rapido
Nouvelle London	Metro-Pol	Cuisine of the Fields
Nouvelle Peasant	Cal-Tex	Nouvelle Facile
Tex-Mex	Greco-Tex	Nouvelle Bistro
Mex-Tex	Ill-Greco	Nouvelle Alimentaire
	Nouveau Mexicano	Cuisine Comique
	Nouveau Americano	
	Cuisine Interruptus	

Key to Abbreviations

Al—Alabama
Cal—California
Chi—Chicago
Chin—Chinese
Ill—Illinois
Juan—Puerto Rico
Kan—Kansas
Mex—Mexican
Miss—Mississippi
Pol—Polish
Swiss—Switzerland
Tex—Texas
Thai—Thailand

*Readers may wish to subscribe to the Leslie Goodman report, a monthly newsletter that tracks the constantly changing types and styles of cooking around the world.

PART II
HOW TO EAT OUT

"Say, I'll bet this is a good place to eat."

> *If all people who eat out a lot are called gourmets, and I eat out a lot, then I am a gourmet.*
>
> Marcel du Goût

4

IDENTIFYING THE REAL GOURMET RESTAURANT

If you are to become a true gourmet, you must know how to eat out. As we all know, dining in a Real Gourmet Restaurant can be a dismaying experience, and the very thought of coping with the *affaire d'haute cuisine* can prompt a squadron of butterflies to attack the strongest of stomachs. Even those of us who eat in these temples of food on a regular basis are not immune to the farfalla that attack our stomach when we cross the threshold of Chez La La Restaurant.

We are not talking about Gourmet-Style, or Pseudo-Gourmet restaurants; we are talking about Real Gourmet. What places a restaurant in the Real Gourmet category? Price, location, snobbery, ambience,* and puffy all go into the makeup. Then there are the dress and accents of the help and, of course, the recommendations of friends: "You must go to Chez La La; it's a

**Ambience* is a certain aura that envelops a restaurant, door to door and wall to wall—a social setting. Food critics use this word a lot when writing about an expensive restaurant. The term is seldom used, except in a snide way, when describing a Greek or Mexican spot or a hot dog stand. I feel, however, that a hot dog stand can have ambience too—like beauty, it's in the eye of the beholder.

Real Gourmet Restaurant." This may be true or may not, depending on who your friends are. (Do *they* know the difference between Pseudo-Gourmet and Real Gourmet?)

The Official Gourmet Handbook wants to help everyone; it will help elevate you to gourmet-quickly-rising-to-epicure status and help to chase away most of those butterflies that are eating your stomach while you are trying to eat Real Gourmet food.

The first thing you need to know is how to distinguish Real Gourmet from the lesser restaurant types. The restaurants that you choose to patronize in your quest for Real Gourmet status are critical. If you waste your money by frequenting nongourmet spots, you will never grasp the true meaning of Real Gourmet in its purest form.

You must expose yourself, selectively, exclusively, and constantly, to Real Gourmet restaurants—nothing else. To frame a perspective for you, I have listed a number of characteristics connected with those restaurants classified as nongourmet.

★ ★ ★ ★ ★

It is not a real gourmet restaurant if . . .

the menu includes disclaimers such as "Not responsible for steaks ordered well done" or "Not responsible for personal property."
wine bottles are hanging from the walls or ceilings.
there is any type of place mat—paper, plastic, rattan, cork.
there's a quiz or games on the place mat.
the forks have bent tines.
the water is served in a water glass like those you use at home.
the wine list is on the back of the menu.
a salad and a choice of potato come with the entrée.
a woven plastic basket of crackers and breadsticks is placed on the table.
the butter is encased in paper or foil that reads "butter."
the plates are not oversized.
the napkins are anything other than cloth.
the candle on the table is in a red pear-shaped globe and the globe is covered with plastic netting.
there are no flowers on the table.
the flowers on the table are artificial.
the lighting is not subdued

there is a neon sign on the outside.
there is anything neon inside.
the floor is covered with shag or industrial carpeting.
the background music is coming from an FM radio station.
there is no tablecloth.
the waiter says, "what'll it be?"
the waiter is a waitress.
you're asked if you want coffee with the entrée.
espresso is not available.
the salad is served in a woven plastic, rattanlike bowl.
the salad greens consist of iceberg lettuce.
freshly ground pepper is not offered.
there is a salad bar.
the menu is food-stained.
there's a big gray plastic tub full of dirty dishes next to your table.
your table allows you enough room to read a newspaper.
there are tables near the kitchen door.
any "cooking" is done in the dining room.
the menu has this note: "all our baked goods are made on the premises."
you see a cash register.
you hear dishes clatter.
you see a bar with stools.
menus are placed on the table instead of in your hand.
you are asked, "Are you ready to order yet?" when your cocktail is served.
you hear the person next to you emit a burp.
you see any men not wearing jackets.
they don't take American Express cards.
the menu states, "15 percent is automatically added to the check for parties of six or more."
the check is presented before you ask for it.
the lighting is bright enough to read the menu.
you can see the street. (Overlooking a garden or park is OK, however.)
you have to light your own candle.
you are offered a choice of salad dressings—one of which is creamy French.
there is a surcharge for Roquefort cheese in a salad dressing.
the menu states, "All of our meals are cooked to order, and good food takes time."
the menu states, "Not responsible for hats and coats."
directions (and a picture) of how to perform The Heimlich Maneuver are posted on the wall next to your table.

5

THE PRELIMINARIES

Making Reservations

Make a reservation to eat out. That's easy! You pick up the phone, call Chez La La, and state what time you wish to experience its culinary delights: "Saturday night at 8:00 P.M. for two people." The person who takes the reservations in a Real Gourmet restaurant has been skillfully trained not to collapse into hysterical laughter when requests like that are made. Rather, he or she will say: "Did you say Saturday night at 8:00 P.M.?" (Pause.) "This Saturday?" (Pause.) "Let me see." (Pause.) "I am sorry; the only thing I have available is after 10:30."

You are crushed, hurt; you feel rejected. Everytime you call a Real Gourmet Restaurant it's the same situation. Don't worry. There's more than one way to beat an egg. We went for advice to Jean-Claude Poulet, a maître d' of some standing (for many years) at Chez Mirage, a restaurant of some standing.

I posed some questions to M. Poulet on the subject of reservations and the problem of getting a certified reservation in a Real Gourmet Restaurant.

Q. *What's the problem with getting a reservation in a Real Gourmet restaurant on a Friday or Saturday night?*
A. Generally speaking, there are never any seats available in any decent, Real Gourmet spot on Friday or Saturday night—*ever!*

Q. *But that's absurd! Are you saying that if I called several weeks in advance, I still could not get a reservation?*
A. This is true. Reservations for *any* Friday or Saturday night, regardless of the lead time, are impossible. The fact of the matter is that there are never any seats available on those nights—that's a standing rule in every Real Gourmet Restaurant.

Q. *Are you telling me that, if I call Chez Mirage and ask for a Friday or Saturday night reservation eight months from now, nothing will be available?*
A. Yes, that is true. Lead time has nothing to do with it.

Q. *Why? For heaven's sake, they can't be that popular!*
A. It has nothing to do with popularity. The standing rule in a Real Gourmet Restaurant is that there is never anything available between the hours of 7:00 P.M. and 10:30 P.M. on Friday and Saturday nights.

Q. *But you said you were going to give us advice on how to beat the reservations runaround. What's your advice?*
A. It is simple. Don't try to make a reservation for Friday or Saturday; go on Tuesday.

Q. *But what if I don't want to go on Tuesday?*
A. *C'est* problem!

Q. *OK. What if I called the maitre d' at Chez La La on Friday at 6:00 P.M. and said, "I'd like a table for two for 8:00 tonight, and I've got $50 that says you can take care of me." What then?*
A. First of all, there are no tables for two in a Real Gourmet restaurant during prime time. *Deux, c'est* tacky!

Q. *No tables for two? That's incredible!*
A. That is correct. Four and six only. Below four is a waste of time; above six causes problems in the kitchen. If you

want a good laugh, try to get a reservation for one person, and a deeper laugh if that one is a woman.

Q. *Then how do these places manage to stay in business?*
A. *C'est simple!* They go for dollars, not volume. A Real Gourmet Restaurant, with the proper exorbitant pricing, and "extras" added in, needs only twenty to thirty people a week to make it.

Q. *Twenty or thirty and they make money? Incredible.*
A. *Mais oui.* Jean Banque-Franc, the owner of Le Gros Franc restaurant, serves fewer than that, and he has many houses, many cars, many boats, many women, and a wife.

Q. *You're kidding! How is that possible?*
A. You have an American saying: "There's a lollipop born every minute."

Q. *You mean there's a* sucker *born every minute, don't you?*
A. Yes, those help too.

M. Poulet was not as much help as I hoped he would be. He did give some advice, however. Go on Tuesdays or open your own Real Gourmet Restaurant.

The Just-Show-Up Ploy

This can be an effective way to eat out without making a reservation. The problem is that it doesn't work in a Real Gourmet spot. It may work in a Gourmet-Style or Pseudo-Gourmet place, if you're willing to "pass some green" (see Chapter 10 on tipping).

In a Gourmet-Style restaurant you will be directed to "have a drink at the bar." This is part punishment (especially if you passed a light green instead of a dark green) and part economics—there's a big markup on booze.

After an appropriate stint

at the bar, you will be retrieved and taken to a table. Don't expect the best one in the house; this is part of the punishment meted out for disregard of the rules and for your cockiness for just showing up.

6

AVANT DÎNER

The importance of proper dress in a Real Gourmet Restaurant cannot be stressed too strongly. This couple has obviously spent the necessary time on Real Gourmet attire.

THE ENTRANCE

How you enter a Real Gourmet Restaurant is extremely important. This part of your eating-out experience—the entrance—will set the tone for the rest of the evening.

Preliminary standards have been met: you and those in your party are properly dressed (see photo). You are not being loud; you have a serious look and a tinge of fear around your eyes. Practice the serious look before you leave home; fear will accompany you and intensify when you and the maître d'[1] lock eyeballs.

Here is how to handle the matter from this point on, and how to disarm even the *hautiest* maître d'.

1. *maître d'* (mat′·er·de′) also means *headwaiter*. It has been shortened—in the United States—from *maître d'hotel*. A maître d' must possess many qualities. Those are, as outlined in *Le Guide Pour la Maître d':* leadership, authority, courtesy, diplomacy, tact, and big pockets. He must also know food and wine and be fluent in several accents.

You will use the well-known tactical maneuver—"the best defense is a good offense"—in this situation. This maneuver is also known as the "maître d' challenge." This is how it works: two hours or so before your scheduled reservation time, call the restaurant and get the name of the maître d' (first name is the best). If you already know his name, skip the above step and those to follow, as you are obviously on your way to becoming an epicure, and you don't need this advice. It doesn't hurt to review procedure once in a while, though.

Armed with the name of the maître d', your fear should lessen a bit, and your palms should dry up slightly.

As you enter the restaurant,[2] do not shake hands, acknowledge, or start the "maître d' challenge" with the first uniformed person you see. (As a point of information, there are very few maîtresses d', so we are dealing primarily with the male of this species.) You must make a confirmed sighting of the maître d' (see photo).

The maître d' will be awaiting your arrival—with a smile—upon your next visit to a Real Gourmet Restaurant.

In a Real Gourmet spot the only person authorized to greet and seat you is the maître d'. A smiling Cantinflas in a white half-apron is not the maître d', nor are those men in the shiny, tired-looking tuxedos. Proceed slowly, and wait until you are officially greeted by the maître d'.

2. If you have coats to check, they will be taken at this point. They *must* be surrendered; outer coats are not allowed in the dining area. They will be cared for: fur coats are put in the walk-in cooler; other coats are cleaned while you are eating. An important point: don't stand around like the "Rube of Burbia" waiting for a coat check—a Real Gourmet Restaurant won't use them.

As you approach the maître d', try to fashion a reasonable smile—not a big grin, just a reasonable, sincere smile. Do not go for a handshake (especially if your hand is empty of green). You can now start the "maître d' challenge." Greet the maître d' by saying, "Ah, good evening, Pierre. Nice to see you again. How have you been?" This will immediately set him back—you know his name, but he doesn't know yours. He will presume that you are a regular customer and will be going through mental chastisement for not remembering who you are. Already you have him by his sweetbreads. Don't let up the attack. "You remember my wife Fiona and her sister Fidelia and Fidelia's husband Percy." Now you really have him against the velvet ropes. Here comes the knockout punch that will have him on the plush carpeting: "Pierre, the last time we were here you gave us an excellent table. Is it possible to get the same one?" Voilà! You're home free. You will, later in the evening, foggily recall that most of your fear left and your palms dried up during this exchange. You will be shown to a nice table and be the recipient of a great deal of bowing (a maître d' does not scrape—don't look for it).

Through all this your companion, or your guests, will be justly impressed with your *savoire faire* and will relate to others what a Real Gourmet you are. Others will tell others, and before you can say "*moules marinière*," your gourmet reputation will precede you whereever you go.

TABLE SELECTION

If you have successfully pulled off the "maître d' challenge," you should get a good table; otherwise, the table selected for you is simply a matter of whimsy on the part of the maître d'. It is generally believed that there is some well-defined strategy that is used to determine where you will be seated—available waiters, traffic flow, time, number of people—when, in fact, it's just plain whimsy.

If you don't like the table that was whimsied upon you, ask for a different one—you won't get it, but you can ask. You won't be able to eat in that restaurant again, and you will probably be made to feel like a banana at an avocado convention, but you can ask. It seems unfair that seat selections can be arranged in airplanes, theaters, and at sporting events but not in restaurants. Why shouldn't paying customers have the right to choose their own seats in a restaurant?

The next time you call for a reservation, specify which table you want: "There will be two of us, but we'd like a table for four; we like lots of room."[1] Or specify "something quiet but away from the service door." Requests like those will put you on the restaurant blacklist and probably rule out even Tuesday reservations. Once you are seated, you have desterilized that table, and it can't be used again for 24 hours, so don't go for a table change. Table change requests must be made prior to sitting down. Don't ask questions like "Could we sit here for just a minute to get the feel of the table to see if we like it?" Once you are seated your chance of getting moved to another table is equal to the possibility of getting a second helping of duck at La Tour d'Argent.

I have a friend who committed several seating *faux pas* at a Real Gourmet spot—selecting his own table, asking for a change (twice). The ploys he has used to try to eat there again have been imaginative—disguising himself as an Arab oil shiek, using the *Tootsie* approach, shaving off his hair and wearing a monocle—but all have met with little success. Now he would take any table (even in the Siberia section), but his efforts have been futile.

Every restaurant has an area designated (by the staff) as Siberia.[2] This is where you will be seated if your mode of dress is considered (by the maître d') to be below the standards of the restaurant; if your companion—a woman—is a real bimbo; if your companion—a man—is wearing a striped polyester suit; if you didn't whisper your name to the maître d' when you entered; if anyone in the party is being loud. (Loud in a Real Gourmet restaurant is not the same as loud in The House of

1. Whatever the number in your party, it's important that you don't blow your *savoir faire* cover by fussing over who sits where. To overcome this obstacle, see Felipe Camel-Back's advice in the footnote on page 109.

2. The Siberia section is made up of tables that are in the lowliest part of the restaurant: near the kitchen door or the serving stations, the farthest away, most nonvisible tables in the room. You cannot see anything or be seen by anybody.

Banquette seating has been the cause of more cases of whiplash than the common fender-bender.

Ribs. The voice level used at a wake is what you should use here.)

Now then, there is some question about the legality of banquette seating and the credibility of a restaurant that is packed with them. If the maître d' is leading you toward a banquette, try to head him off before he gets you there. Your evening, without a doubt, will be ruined if you end up in one of those glorified Greyhound bus seats. Banquette seating has many problems: you sit too low in relation to the table so your line of vision is obstructed by the wine glasses; the table traps you in for the entire evening and you can't go to the rest room; there is a magical Velcro attraction between banquette fabric and a woman's dress; they cause stiff necks—eat, turn your head, talk, eat, turn your head. Take note of people seated in a banquette—sheer misery stuffed between the ears (see photo). The situation becomes more ludicrous when two men are seated side by side in a banquette; that's no way for grown men to eat. Use any excuse you can think of to avoid banquette seating—bad back, short legs, long legs, allergy to velour, kidney problems. There will be more than enough problems to deal with; eliminating this one will certainly help the evening go a bit smoother.

ORDERING

Preprandial Drinks

After being seated you will

be approached by a different uniform from that which seated you; this person is known as a captain (see photo). In the restaurant pecking order he is second in command. (To keep the record straight, there are no female captains, nor are there co-captains.) Multiroomed restaurants have a captain for each room; they are known as *room captains*. The captain will say, "Good evening. May I get you a cocktail?"

Digression is called for here. The *cocktail*—a word used millions and millions of times every day. What is the etymology of the word? You may not like the answer, but here it is:

The primitive cocktail of the Manhattan pioneers consisted of cocks' tails dipped in a concoction of pimientos, with which they tickled their throats to incite them to drink.

Maybe that should read "the pioneer cocktail of the primitive Manhattans."

The ordering of a cocktail doesn't mesh with the glamour or expense of an important gourmet meal. So, in a Real Gourmet Restaurant you should skip the cocktail and order an aperitif. The captain will spot a trace of discernment about you, if you say, "No cocktails for us. We would like an aperitif—a Kir or a vintage brut champagne, well chilled." With that pronouncement, you will have earned the respect of the captain (and cer-

This is the captain in a Real Gourmet Restaurant. He's a rung below the maître d' on the restaurant ladder, but don't underestimate his power: he decides who looks the most important at your table and therefore, who gets the menu with the prices.

tainly the respect of the others around you). The custom in a Real Gourmet spot is to have (and be offered) only one preprandial drink. This is especially true if you have eschewed the aperitif route and taken the side road to oblivion—the extra-dry martini.

Real Gourmet restaurants have little tolerance with overt gin guzzlers. In fact, many restaurants foist their "kitchen mistakes" onto customers who have the audacity to immobilize their taste buds with gin. The restaurant feels, and rightfully so, that you have no taste—literally or otherwise. So why should you be served the very best?

On the other hand, wine can be consumed before, during, and after the meal, and wine drinking is encouraged cork after cork.

The Menus

The next major event to take place is the handing out of the menus. As everyone knows, the object of a menu is to list the dishes that the restaurant has to offer, along with their prices. But in some gourmet spots there are two sets of menus—one with prices and one without prices. As things go, the person who looks the most important gets the menu with the prices. If only one man and one woman are at the table, the man will get the priced menu. This sangfroid approach has given rise to a few sex discrimination suits.[1]

The Daily Specials

Next comes the recitation by the captain of the "daily specials."[2] (Daily specials are a ploy used by restaurants that don't feel comfortable with the food listed on the menu. More importantly, the price of the specials is never revealed until you look at the check—you'll need your Gold Card to settle this one. It's certainly putting a bit of polish on

1. In the case of Billy "The Whip" Belmonte vs. Ristorante Cavatelli a famous jockey sued the restaurant because the menu with the prices was given to his chorus-girl friend (the captain thought he was her son). The judge, ruling in favor of the plaintiff, said, "Captains should not hand out priced menus on a presumed basis; they must first determine who's getting stuck with the tab."

2. In a Real Gourmet restaurant the words *daily specials* are often replaced by more expensive words like *les spur du moment, les plats à moi, les idées s'amuser, les spécialités du plat bleu, le prix secret.*

the lily for a place that boasts an eight-page menu to offer ten to twelve daily specials—from soup to dessert—in addition. Points can be curried from the captain, and the kitchen, if you choose one or more of the specials rather than order from the menu. There is a subtle intimation that the specials are fresh and *au courant;* the everyday dishes on the menu are musty, and the chef doesn't like to cook them.

Using his deepest accent—French, Italian, etc.—the captain will run through these recent and marvelous creations from the kitchen. Don't try to understand what he is saying; it's not important. But you must be courteous and attentive to his recitation; anything less than rapt attention is a serious gaffe. Be alert, nod your head knowingly, mumble back-of-the-throat words; get off a few remarks like "That sounds delicious," and mutter some *mmmmmm*s. When the captain is finished he will ask, "Would you like a few minutes to think it over?" You then nod your head in a "yes" direction.

(Some restaurants have taken to listing the specials on a mini-menu and leaving it on the table after the recitation. Real [and serious] Gourmet spots will not do this. They like to see you dangle in the wind.)

When the captain returns to take your order, ask him to recite the specials again; ask him to explain sauces, accompaniments, freshness, the origin of the dish, and the price. Notice two things in particular this time: his obvious distress and his not-so-deep accent. Ask for a few more minutes to decide. In the meantime, peruse the menu like good gourmets. In a Macro-Gourmet Restaurant the menu will list the dishes in a language that you are probably not fluent in; and no English translation will be given. In a Micro-Gourmet Restaurant the English translation will follow the exotic-sounding foreign words.

If there are no English translations on the menu, "call" the captain to your table.[3] Ask him to translate into English every dish listed on the menu.

3. Calling the captain is not done in the same way as, say, calling your dog. In a Macro-Gourmet Restaurant you don't call anybody—not even your baby-sitter. The proper way to "call" the captain is this: first, you catch his eye, then, you blink once or twice while nodding your head. Don't raise your hand, yell out, or be loud or obtrusive in any way (see photo).

Don't "call" the captain the way you'd hail a cab. This man is making a fool of himself by rising from the table to get the captain's attention.

Would you dive into a pool without knowing the depth of the water?

I should point out one anomaly connected with the daily-special recitation and the menu listings. This abnormality is known as the "showing of the food" (or should it be "showing off the food"?). Here are two examples of this phenomenon:

•

Real Gourmet Restaurant. At this place the daily specials are not only verbalized, but you get to eye them at the same time—sort of a food show-and-tell. Samples of all the specials, from soup to dessert, are brought to the table for inspection. You actually get to *see* the *Pâté de Canard d'Amiens,* the *Médaillons de*

Example A

Pollo Arrosto al Forno con Rosmarino

(Translation) (Roast Chicken with Rosemary)

Example B

Potage DuBarry ou Crème de Chou-Fleur

(Translation) (Cauliflower Soup)

Volaille à la Mantouane, etc, etc. Why anyone would want to "inspect" a raw chicken breast is beyond me. (It's what the damn chef does with it that matters.) Some places need these culinary fireworks to dazzle your eyes with the hope of defusing your taste buds.

●

Pseudo-Gourmet Steak and Lobster Restaurant. Here the food is brought to the table in its natural state. A selection of raw steaks—dripping blood or turning gray—are brought to be waked before their delivery to the hot coals of the kitchen grill. Live lobsters, their ominous claws snapping the pellucid air, antennae weaving a frightful dance of death, are perversely thrust under your nose—a macabre way to start a meal. However, any resemblance to what you saw and what you eventually get is purely coincidental.

Types of Menus

À La Carte. Also known as *carte du jour* or *carte du ruin.* The price of each dish, from appetizer to dessert, is priced separately on the menu. In a Real Gourmet spot, where the cuisine is *haute,* so are the prices. The total, in this case, definitely equals the sum of the parts. It is best to do some quick addition in your head before you foolishly forge ahead through five or six courses; this could lead to a "check aftershock" that you will feel down to your toes.

●

Prix Fixe (pree·fee). This is a fixed-price menu. A fixed-price menu is intended to include everything from appetizer to dessert—the whole smear. However, you should be aware of the hidden "extras." Sometimes the *up* charge for certain dishes is listed on the menu, and sometimes it is not. For example, the *Pâté de Maison* (meat loaf) will be included in the fixed price, whereas *Escargots Anciennes* carries a surcharge of, say, $2.50. Generally speaking, uninteresting appetizers, salads, entrées, and desserts, will be included in the fixed price; more exotic and interesting dishes will carry a surcharge.

●

Table d'Hôte. This means the *table of the host.* This type of menu is the same as the *prix fixe.*

●

Dégustation (dis·gust′·ing). The definition is: to taste attentively so as to perceive flavor.

This type of dinner is an endless succession of courses of food; each course suffers from cuisine anemia; the courses are small, small, small. Many people go from a *dégustation* dinner straight to a pizza place for added sustenance. It's a fixed meal all the way: the prices are fixed, and so are the courses—you have no choice either way. People who are pseudo-gourmets revel in *dégustation* dinners even though they don't know what they're eating and they can't begin to pronounce the fancy words attached to, and liberally sprinkled over, the dishes served.

7

DINING ETIQUETTE—*CHEZ LA LA STYLE*

TABLE MANNERS

The manners-for-the-gourmet rules should not be passed over lightly. This is not the time to go with the "rules were meant to be broken" philosophy. Rules of the table are like the rules of the road—if you disobey them, your chances of survival are nil to zero. The patrons—and the staff—in a Real Gourmet Restaurant do not tolerate people who are fork offenders, lip smackers, napkin tuckers, or who usually eat in family-style restaurants. Your station in life will be determined by how high your social graces stack up and how carefully you adhere to the following rules.

Napkins

The minute you are seated, unfold and place the cloth napkin in your lap. (All Real Gourmet Restaurants use cloth napkins.) If you fail to do this, the captain will do it for you, in an embarrassing bullfighterlike fashion. As you are

This diner won't even reach the first step in his climb toward Real Gourmet status if he continues to tuck his napkin into his collar (to say nothing of hoisting his soup bowl off the table while eating from it).

unfolding the napkin, inspect it for crispness, worn edges, stains, small holes, etc. Should you find the napkin unacceptable for any reason, ask for another. This will get you off to a real good start with the captain.

During the course of the meal, try not to use the napkin to wipe your mouth. A perfunctory dab in the general direction of your eating orifice is acceptable; a heavy wipe of your mouth and nose is a clear sign of crudity.

Never tuck the napkin into your shirt collar. The accompanying photo shows the masculine mode of dress, as I have never seen a woman try this—even those who wear shirt collars. However, a woman with a shirt collar shouldn't be eating in a Real Gourmet Restaurant anyway. Napkin tucking is a juvenile approach to eating; it sends up a flag that says you are a sloppy eater or you're still learning how to eat. If you insist on employing this bib approach (which is better left to, and is acceptable in, lobster and rib joints), don't be surprised if the captain makes remarks like "Well, how's the little fellow doing this evening?" or "Gosh, I'm sorry, but our barber has the night off."

At the conclusion of the meal, carefully fold the napkin into the shape of a butterfly and place it to the left of where your plate was (napkins should not be removed from the lap until all plates are removed from the table). By no means should you place the napkin in a dirty plate or on the right.

Table Setting

Always give the table a good *coup d'oeil.* Check the tablecloth for stains or wear and make sure it is centered on the table with the proper overhang on all sides. Ask to have the cloth changed if you detect any of these faults. Next, examine the silver and the glassware for spots and stains; ask for immediate replacement of those that are sullied. Don't clean anything with your napkin or the end of the tablecloth; you're eating out, not pulling KP.

Take note of silverware placement: forks should be on your left (except the fish fork, which will be on your right). Knives and spoons will be on your right (the sharp edge of the knife should be facing the plate). The butter plate should be to your left, three inches above the forks; the butter knife should be at the top edge of the plate, on a horizontal plane. Water and wine glasses should be at the top and to the right of the service plate, three and one-half inches from the tip of the spoons.[1]

If your inspection reveals any deviation from the above description, "call" the captain and have the necessary corrections or adjustments made.

Review the illustration, reprinted from the *Gourmet's Guide to Table Inspection* pamphlet, to confirm accuracy.[2]

1. Some Real Gourmet spots will not set the table as described and shown on page 46. Appropriate knives and forks will be brought with each course, so don't start asking for "missing" pieces, or the entire restaurant staff will do a turn-up-nose symphony in your honor.
2. You might wish to make a photocopy of the picture to take along to the restaurant to ensure total compliance.

SILVER SPOTTING GUIDE

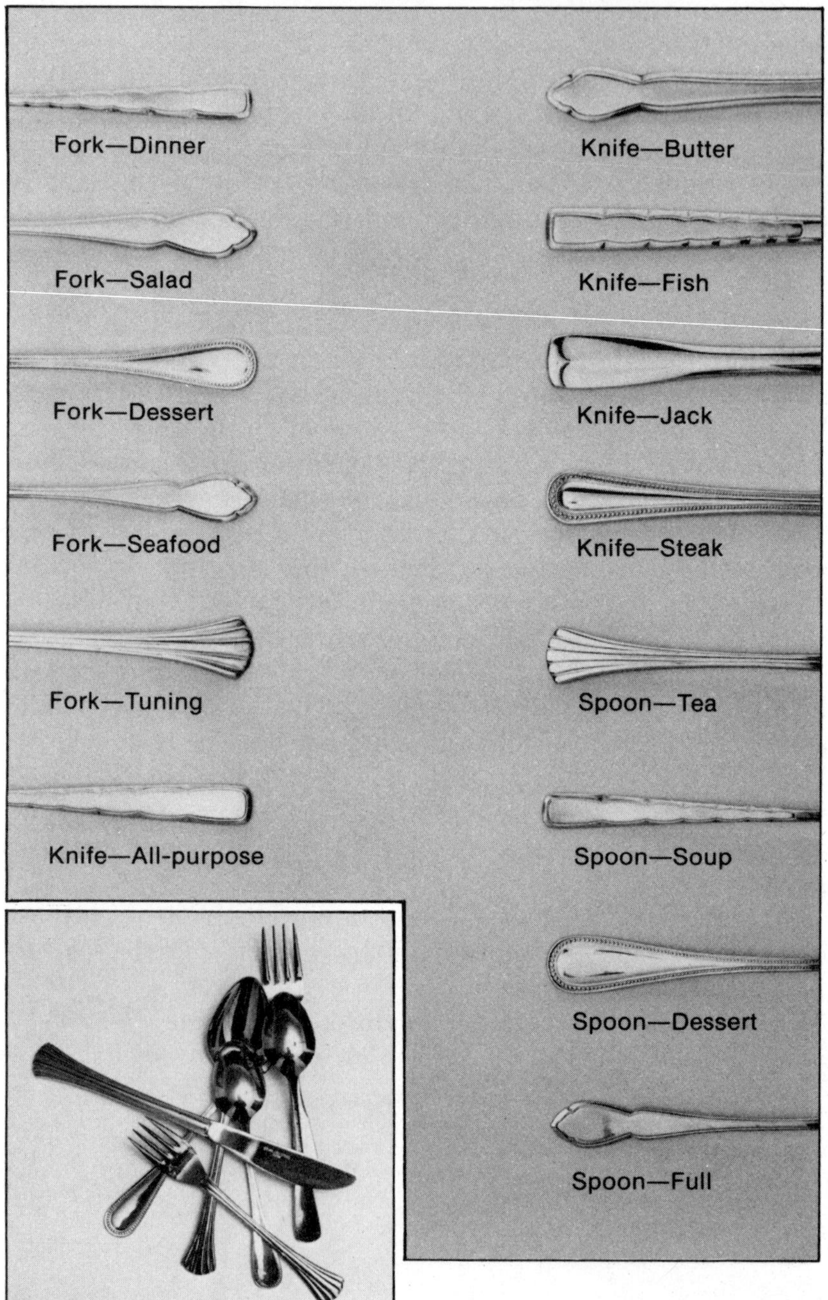

Silverware Selection

The famous (and often botched) theory, known as "outside to inside," whereby the utensils farthest from the plate are used first, is no longer valid. It is quite unwise, therefore, to set out in this direction as you begin to traverse through courses of food; without question, you will wind up on the short end of a salad fork.

Research conducted at the famous Hotel Training School, Ecole de Pesche, near Plattsburgh, New York, has shown that people who eat out on a regular basis would prefer to deal with one fork and one knife throughout the meal rather than be anxious about proper selection of utensils for the various foods served. In fact, the research showed that most people saw nothing wrong with licking off the fork or knife between courses. The research also revealed that people at formal dinners and those who eat in Real Gourmet restaurants are frozen with fear when they see a table laden with a multitude of forks, knives, and spoons of every shape and size.

The most common complaint voiced by those surveyed was that there are no basic standards for size and shape, no pattern or consistency; every restaurant or dinner presents a whole new set of problems. Of course, you can always follow the lead of the host or hostess or someone at the table that you trust. Well, that's less-than-original thinking and usually doesn't work. What if you can't see which utensil the host or hostess is using? What if there's no one at the table that you trust? What if there's only you and that little trixie that you're trying to impress?

There is only one foolproof method for selecting the right utensil at the right time. The illustrated manual *Another Place, Another Tine,* written by Constance Goldenrod with Comtesse de Billy, is a priceless reference book for everyone who eats. Needless to say, it chases away the clouds that line the silver and makes it simple for everyone to understand utensil usage.

UTENSIL-WIELDING STYLES

Salary of less than $8,000 annually.

Salary of $8,000–$20,000 annually.

Permission has been granted from the publisher to reprint portions of the chapter "Silverware Spotting and Other UFOs."*

*Extra copies of the Silver Spotting Guide on page 46 (laminated for easy cleaning), suitable for taking to restaurants and formal dinners, are available for $.25 each. Send to: HI-HO ARGENTO, PO Box 1212, Cleveland, OH 48234. Special quantity discounts are available to gourmet clubs.

Salary of $20,000–$50,000 annually.

Salary of more than $50,000 annually.

Utensil Wielding

How you use your knife and fork at the table is directly connected to gross annual income. Only one of the following pictures shows correct knife and fork usage. Can you pick out the right one? How can you expect to achieve Real Gourmet status if you can't handle a knife and fork in the accepted manner?

GENERAL RULES

Here are some basic rules that cover an *omnium-gatherum* of situations that one might face when eating out.

All gourmet meals, or meals of importance, have a natural order of progression. Here, for example, is a meal—a proper one at that—served on the occasion of the 10th anniversary of Vinnie's Pit-Stop Spot Diner (exit 84D, New York State Thruway). Notice the logical succession of courses: appetizer, soup, fish course, meat course, and *la touche finale.*

Caviar Beluga
Malossol

•

Consommé de Gibier

•

Truite Saumonée,
Sauce Hollandaise

•

Pommes à la
Steameur

•

Suprême de Poularde
a l'Espagnole

•

Mousse Glacée à la
Favorite

•

Mignardises

Naturally, the appropriate wines were served with each course. Vinnie's chef, Nunzio, struck a serious offkey note in the composition of the menu by not serving a *coup du milieu* (sherbet) between the fish and the chicken; otherwise, it was one fine meal, so they say. In the process of selecting courses for a meal, keep in mind Vinnie's menu and order accordingly.

Never ask questions like "Does this come with potatoes and a salad?" or "What kind of salad dressings do you have?" or "Are the vegetables fresh or canned?"

Restaurants do not like arrhythmic ordering: if two people are dining, two appetizers must be ordered; if only one person orders an appetizer, the rhythm of the meal gets bouncy. If one person wants the salad before the entrée, and another wants it after the entrée, the measured beat of the meal will go haywire—not to mention what it will do to the kitchen. *Everyone at the table should stay in step when ordering*—appetizer, appetizer; soup, soup; salad, salad, and so forth.

If you follow the pattern of Vinnie's anniversary meal, there will be no problem in ordering wine: white wine—a Chevalier-Montrachet 1979—would do justice to the salmon. A Saint-Emilion 1970 or 1976 is a perfect complement to the poularde, as the lightness of this fine red wine totes well with the Espagnole sauce. Problems arise in the ordering of wine when this one is having fish, this one is having meat, this one is having chicken. The choice of red wine or white wine becomes a weighty problem. One bottle of white wine for the fish eaters may be too much; one bottle of red wine for the meat eaters may not be enough. The problem is compounded by the fact that there are no half-bottles of wine any more; the species became extinct some time ago. Rosé is not the answer—I've yet to meet a good Rosé wine. Wine by the glass is not the solution. Real Gourmet Restaurants are usually not kind enough to offer that option; and those that might, serve the dregs of the bin. The solution is this: everyone at the table must order the same type of food—majority must rule. Those refusing to switch should be asked to leave the table.

Once the captain is poised tableside, ready to take your order, no hesitation is permitted. Everyone must order promptly and efficiently. If the flow of ordering is stopped because of indecision, the captain will leave, and the silver butter dish will turn green before he is seen again.

The table is yours for the evening—that's a cardinal rule in any temple of haute cuisine. Take the time to savor and enjoy the food and drink—and your fellow gourmets. A true gourmet spot doesn't need to use the table more than once an evening, so even if you eat early, say at 6:00, feel free to keep the table until 10:00 or 11:00. You have, in a manner of speaking, rented that table for the evening. Look at it this way: when you rent a car you keep it until you are through with it; someone doesn't stop you in the middle of the road and tell you that your time is up, that someone else is waiting for that car. It's the same with your table—you don't have to give it up. If other people are waiting for a table, then the restaurant is guilty of overbooking; they should stew in their own juices.

The question of whether or not ashtrays, silver, peppermills, napkins, etc., should be "appropriated" is perplexing to many people. A basic *regola empirica* is this: anything that has the restaurant's name, initials, or crest is fair game. Restaurants expect you to take these mementos—that's how they advertise!

It is well inside the fences that define the boundaries of etiquette for a lady to give her order directly to the captain and not have it relayed by the gentleman. In fact, most women resent having a man play the Charlie McCarthy role. Exceptions to this are: if the woman is drunk; if she doesn't speak well; if she has a high-pitched voice; or, if she tries to pronounce the foreign words on the menu.

Condiments, such as ketchup, mustard, A-1 sauce, etc., will not be available in a Real Gourmet Restaurant. It may be wise to put a few plastic packets of these (pick them up free at most fast-food joints) in your pocket or purse and have them with you should they be needed.

Sacs du canine (doggie bags), are usually not available. The reasons: if the food is edible, you'll eat it all, because you won't get a whole lot to eat; if it's not edible, you won't want to take it home anyway. Also, dishes such as *suprême de volaille à la crème noisette* doesn't travel well in a doggie bag. You may choose, however, to bring with you some plastic food bags, just in case there are some extra petit fours, rolls, fruit, etc.

Do not, I repeat, *do not,* commit the unforgivable sin of asking to split a dish. The wrath of the captain will envelop your table like a giant butterfly net. "Split! Split! How can I split a Queues d'Écrevisses en Timbales Nantua?" he will ask, as his voice cranks up to the choirboy level. So, unless you're ready to have a big red *R* (for *rube*) stamped on your table, don't bring up the subject of splitting.*

Cigarette or cigar smoking is perfectly acceptable in any

*You can, of course, split the dishes on your own or taste from each other's plate. This will leave you open to ocular abuse from the captain, but they're like that anyway.

type of gourmet restaurant and should be fully enjoyed. Some tips on this:

- Never light your own; this is the responsibility of the captain or one of his staff.
- Don't extinguish your cigarette or cigar in anything except an ashtray.
- Smoke only between courses, not during.
- Don't sample a wine with smoke in your mouth.
- If someone near you is offended by your smoking, ask the captain to move the complainer to another table.

To claim that wines should not be changed is a heresy; the palate becomes saturated and after the third glass the best of wines arouses nothing but an obscure sensation.

Brillat-Savarin
The Physiology of Taste (1825)

8

WINE SELECTION

Selecting a wine is not at all like selecting a car. When selecting a car to purchase, you can kick the tires, look under the hood, sit in the driver's seat, and take it for a test spin. You can't put a wine through the same thumping, even though some wines are priced about the same as a Ford Pinto, so there is a bit of injustice here. The information that follows should help to minimize potentially gross errors in selecting wines and further your education on the vine. (Use of the wine-tasting chart at the end of Chapter 9 will also be a big help.)

Wine lists can be intimidating, so let's discuss the different types, which range from a single card with a few mediocre selections to elaborate books that read like a pedigree of the vines.

EXAMPLE 1

This is the straightforward, card-type list. It will list eight to ten wines and use short, punchy sentences to describe them. Illustration:

Grave de Ausone—A full-bodied red wine that delivers

HOW TO READ A WINE BOTTLE LABEL

excitement in every sip. Clean, vigorous, persistent, with a subtle aftertaste of coach leather. Recommended with chops, steak, venison, beef stew.

There are a lot of problems to deal with here: What does coach leather taste like? None of the recommended foods will appear on the menu. And what makes a wine clean, vigorous, persistent?

This type of wine list is supplied to the restaurant by a wine distributor who is pushing his own wines. No year will be listed for the wine. This doesn't necessarily make it a bad wine, but don't expect jolts of excitement bursting through your mouth. At the very bottom you will find Sangria by the pitcher, house wines by the carafe, and a cheap Asti Spumante.

EXAMPLE 2

This will be a two-page fold-over with a red imitation plastic cover. The inside pages will have a few grease spots here and there. The list will be sitting on the table, stuck in between the salt and pepper shakers and the sugar-packet holder. The list will include French, Italian, German, California, Australian, and Hungarian selections. Four or five will be listed for each country, except for the Hungarian, which will include only two as that country has only two. The only wines that will list a year (known as a *vintage*), will be the French and California offerings. Descriptions on this type of list are brief and to the point. There will be no guide as to food and wine compatability, so you are on your own. There will also be a listing for a cheap Asti Spumante.

EXAMPLE 3

Here we have a fairly large loose-leaf binder with clear plastic leaves. Inserted under the clear plastic are the actual labels of the wines offered (this is a real bush league approach). This type of list suggests that you will be more at ease seeing the actual label; better still, you will recognize an old favorite. The fact of the matter is that this is a cheap way to put together a wine list, and if the restaurant is out of a brand of wine, the label is pulled from the book. This type of list is a big help to some: prom night people, the timid, and people who collect postage stamps.

EXAMPLE 4

This is a leather-bound book that is delivered to your table with solemnity and style by the *sommelier.* It will read like an encyclopedia of wines; the offerings will be deep, the prices steep, and the selections predominantly French. Most of the wines will have a year—this in itself makes for a higher price. This type of list (and restaurant) will expect you to be on your toes. The wine steward/*sommelier* will expect you to flip through the many pages with casual sophistication. You will be expected to make a proper selection relative to the food ordered. This you must do with dispatch and *savoir faire.* And, of course, the wine must be ordered by number—don't forget the number.

■ ■ ■

Those are the predominant types of lists one would be exposed to. There are, however, still others. The esoteric, the cute, the ridiculous, and the self-serving seem to be pushing deeper and deeper into restaurants of all classes. Here are some examples I have seen:

A large piece of wood, nearly the size of a door, on which the wine selections have been carved was offered by a restaurant whose owner is a wood-carving hobbyist. Selection changes keep him rather busy. On several occasions the door has fallen out of the hands of the wine steward and completely wiped out a table for four—food, people, china. . . .

Parchment paper (Dead Sea Scroll type) is rolled on both ends of wooden paper towel holders. This type calls for a lot of manual dexterity. It also calls for a great set of eyes. Unrolling the list, trying to read it by candlelight, stretching the arms far enough to read the entire list without losing control and having the list snap back and eat your hand call for agility—Olympic style.

The blackboard type, with wine selections scrawled on it, is always hung on the wall that is farthest from your table. Binoculars are necessary to make a selection.

The paper place mat type is fun. In addition to the listing of wines, there is usually a game or a quiz. I always worry about the service in a place that has games on the place mat.

Then there is the my-sister-has-good-handwriting type. This adds a personal touch to the wine list but is, in most instances, impossible to decipher. Furthermore, by the time the sister completes the list (she's a tongue-biting writer), the vintage has changed.

To help expand the information on wine selection and to delve into the areas of ordering wine, and wine protocol, we solicited the aid of M. Mouton Cadet, the director of the famous wine institute—Les Sociétés de la Chevrolet Van at Santenay in the Côte de Beaune. Here, then, is some vine advice from M. Cadet:

•

Wines are usually ordered by bin number; the number will be somewhere in the vicinity of the name. Use that number when ordering. The reason for the number is to save the embarrassment of trying to pronounce the name.

•

Feel free to ask for help in selecting a wine. Query the sommelier/*wine steward on areas of doubt. "Which are the reds, the whites?" "Is this wine [point to the name] as dry as a Muscatel, or is it sweet like Cold Duck?" "I was born in 1948. Was that a good year?"*

•

As a rule, house wines are not served in the better restaurants. Don't look for them on the wine list, and don't ask. House wines are usually a jug wine with a screw-top cap. There has never been a quality vintage wine with a screw-top cap. Not yet, that is.

•

Red versus white and the food compatibility question will go on until someone makes a blue wine. A simple rule: white with fish, red with meat, rosé when in doubt, and no wine goes with chocolate.

•

Quality does not always relate to price. There are some very expensive wines that would make one-third of a very expensive salad dressing.

•

If a wine carries a low price, it is probably a bad wine. The exception to this is Italian wines. There are no bad Italian wines—there are no great ones, either.

•

If you order a quality vintage year, you will be on safe ground. But I know of only three people in the world who can recall the top years for Burgundy, Bordeaux, Loire, Médoc, Chablis, Mosels (I am one of them).

•

Do not order an inexpensive wine in a premier restaurant. The sommelier *will deduce that you are cheap. The word will be passed around to the captain, the busboys—and the rooster will be crowing before you finish your meal.*

•

If you do not have a stomach for violence, accept the wine you ordered, even if it is bad. There were only eighteen times in the past several years when a wine was rejected in a Real Gourmet Restaurant. (I hold the distinction of rejecting four wines in one evening.) The flowers my wife sent to the hospital the next day were beautiful.

•

If you think the wine tastes bad, do not ask the opinion

of the wine steward, especially if he is working on commission. He will assure you that "the wine is exactly as it should be" and that's the last you will see of him.

•

It is perfectly all right to carry a small, wallet-sized chart that rates wines by year and country. It's all right to carry it, but never *take it out in public. It is better to write crib notes on your shirt cuff than be guilty of such open ignorance.*

I am tempted to believe that smell and taste are in fact but a single composite sense whose laboratory is the mouth and whose chimney is the nose.

Brillat-Savarin
The Physiology of Taste (1825)

9

WINE TASTING

Despite the fact that, for the past several years, the grape crop has been bumper to bumper on the vine, the price of wine is rising. A query to the wine boards of several countries on the reasons for these escalating prices resulted in mixed answers. Some said, "It's the price of the bottle." Others said, "It's the slow pickers." Some attributed the problem to "greed on the part of the wine merchants and restaurant owners." Whatever the reasons, a good bottle of wine is an important part of a meal, and it helps bad food go down easier. It is important that a sophisticated eater be able to judge a wine properly—important to your pocket and your palate. Besides, how often do you spend big bucks on something you can't pronounce? And then there's all that pomp and circumstance, not to mention *sommelier* intimidation. To aid you through this vineyard courtship, the chart at the end of the chapter should be taken along to the restaurant. Follow the simple directions for testing and scoring. If the wine passes the test, you can be assured of enjoyment. If it flunks, you may be asked to leave. Try to get some rolls and butter into your stomach early on, just in case. (*Note:* Bring some extra copies of the testing chart in case you need them.)

START THE TESTING

Begin with the nose part of the chart.

Raise the glass without disturbing the wine. Stick your nose into the glass. Inhale; concentrate. Don't hold the glass under your nose too long; otherwise the sensations get all mixed up. Rotate the glass to trap the scent in the upper part of the glass (take your nose away first). You are smelling for *intensity.* Select the appropriate words in the first column of your card, then select one of the four numbers given and circle the points. Rotate the glass again and bring it back to your nose. Through deep and spaced inhalations (sort of like hyperventilating), recognize the sensations guided by the words in the second column—*evaluation.* Select the appropriate words and circle the points. Do the same thing for *identifiable aromas*—it's OK if you underline more than one word. Circle the points. Don't forget to concentrate. It's a help if you can close your eyes during this part of the testing.

Now move on to the mouth part of the testing (this is the best part and certainly the most critical).

Take a little of the wine in your mouth and rotate it over your taste buds on the tongue. You can repeat this two or three times. While doing so, concentrate on the characteristics of *balance* and *harmony* and keep an eye on the wine steward (he won't normally carry a gun, but restaurants do have a lot of knives). Underline the appropriate words and assign the points.

Important: Do not swallow!

The *aftertaste* scoring comes next.

With the wine in the mouth, breathe in a little air between closed teeth. *Now swallow!* Compare the sensation with that when the wine was still in the mouth. You're looking for *aromatic persistence* here, so start counting the number of seconds this lasts. Six seconds is short, nine is good, and fourteen is long. (Are you keeping an eye on the wine steward and your dinner companion?) Mark the score.

Now move on to the *eye analysis.*

Hold the glass up to a source of light—candle, chandelier, etc. Underline something under *transparency* and *effervescence.* Swirl the wine in the glass. Examine for arcs (known in fashionable wine circles as *legs*) that form on the side of the glass. Underline something under *texture.* (How are the wine steward and the little lady doing?) Finally, tip the glass against the white tablecloth and check the color. Underline something and circle the numbers.

Add up all the circled numbers.

If the score is nineteen or lower, send back the wine, ask for another bottle, and start over again.

ORDER OF PROCEDURE

1. Ask to see the wine list (for more dope on this, see Chapter 8).
2. If you are in an expensive restaurant, a person (usually a man), with either a gold cluster of grapes on his lapel or a round silver dish hung around his neck (be sure to look for these symbols, as the old saying "busboys don't know nothing about wine" is true) will proffer a wine list.
3. Select a wine (don't forget the numbering system).
4. The *sommelier*/wine steward will present the label for your inspection. Be polite. Glance at the label, nod your head, and mumble something in the direction of "that's fine." He will take out the cork for your inspection. By all means inspect it; it's part of the ritual. It is not necessary to smell the cork; this part of the ritual has become *déclassé.* He will now pour a small amount of wine into your glass.*
5. At this point, take out the testing chart. (Bring your own pen; don't push your luck.)

*Before tasting the wine, your palate and taste buds must be cleansed of any pollution from other alcohols. If your predinner cocktail was a stiff martini, your taste buds are probably hiding behind your tonsils. Coax them back out by eating some bread; otherwise the wine will slide off your tongue and disappear into your stomach without even saying "hello" to your taste buds.

Wine Testing Chart

INTENSITY

strong		*Evaluation*	
persistent		unpleasant	
ample		ethereal	
subtle		fruity	
pronounced		fragrant	
fleeting		refined	
thin		callous	
flat	1	jumpy	1
busty	2	happy	2
	3	grumpy	3
	4	dopey	4

BALANCE, HARMONY

austere	upper-income	
heady	full	
soft	semifull	
strong	good breeding	
pungent		
pure		
simple		
lacking		
mature		
young		
innocent		
virgin		
seductive		
velvety		
mouth-puckering		
elegant		
flabby		
muscular		
symphonic		
green		
ripe		2
overripe		4
		5

QUALITY

Identifiable Aromas	
aspirin	
spice	
bitter lemon	
plum	
apricot	
walnut husks	
hazelnut	
licorice	
underbrush	
fur	
dried fruits	
coffee	
pine trees	
tar pits	
vinegar	
kelp	
new car	
chamois	
ragu	1
forest fire	2
forest tucker	3
sophie tucker	4

AFTER-TASTE

aroma	
aromatic	
persistence	
short	
good	
long	
	2
	4
	5

TRANSPARENCY	EFFERVESCENCE
bright clear cloudy rain cumulus stormy small-craft warnings	fine bubbles medium bubbles large bubbles long bubbles oval bubbles double bubble bubble bath

TEXTURE	LEGS		COLOR	
fluid oily short-waisted full-bodied thin-bodied tap water	average long dynamite	1 2 3	golden straw cherry magenta copper ruby pearl silver tonto lemon ice	1 2 3

Some people are in a bad temper while digestion is in progress; it is therefore not the time either to suggest projects or to ask favors of them.

Brillat-Savarin
The Physiology of Taste (1825)

10

TIPS ON TIPPING

CAPTAINS/MAÎTRES D'

Tipping a maître d' (also known as "the feeling of the green" or "the green handshake") is quite simple. Follow this procedure:

Prior to leaving for the restaurant, prepare the bill of your choice by folding it into a size that will fit nicely into the palm of your hand. Here is how this is done:

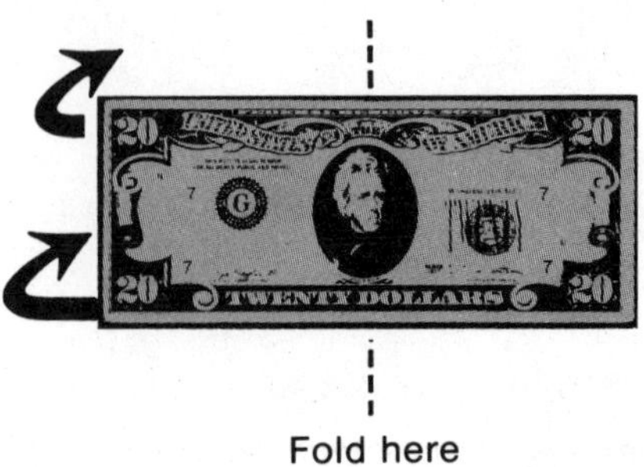

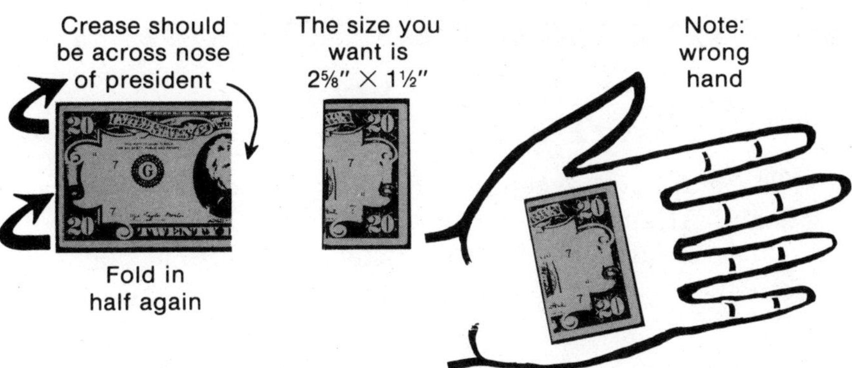

The reason for the fold is twofold: tuxedos have small pockets, and captains/maîtres d' in good restaurants have little time to empty them. (Also, it is much more civilized.)

The Execution

As the captain/maître d' greets you, extend your hand (the one with the palmed bill, usually the right hand). As soon as he "feels the green" he will smile and say, "Nice to see you again." Slide your hand away from his, deftly transferring the money. Restaurant captains/maîtres d' have very sensitive palms; they can, with uncanny accuracy, tell whether it is a five, ten, or twenty without the hint of a look. After he has seated you he will verify the denomination and make an appropriate entry next to your name in his reservation book. (This will determine your seating, service, etc., the next time.)

Don't try a dollar bill or, worse, rolling up two or three dollar bills—he will feel right through you.

That is the accepted method, around the world, for tipping a captain/maître d'.

VARIATION I FOR CAPTAINS/MAÎTRES D'

There are two exceptions to this method—Las Vegas and Atlantic City require a different approach.

First of all, the fold is different. Here is the method:

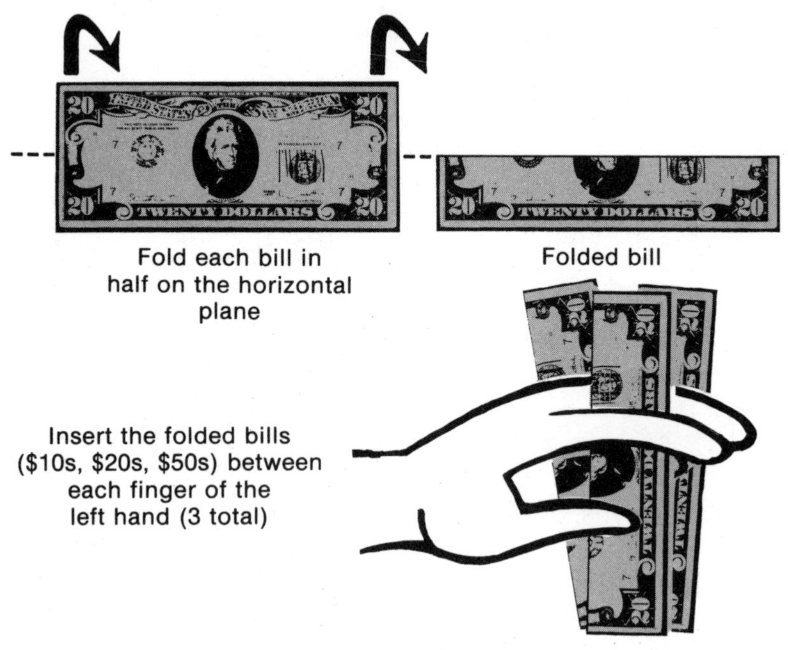

Fold each bill in half on the horizontal plane

Folded bill

Insert the folded bills ($10s, $20s, $50s) between each finger of the left hand (3 total)

The Execution

As you enter, extend your right hand to the captain/maître d'. Have your left hand in front of your body, chest high, with the money displayed prominently. The captain will pluck the bills from your fingers, total them, and check for counterfeits. Do not attempt this method with dollar bills.

ALTERNATE APPROACH: LAS VEGAS, ATLANTIC CITY ONLY

This approach requires no bill folding, but the bill must be in your left hand, it must be perfectly flat (new $50s work great), and ready to go.

The Execution

You will start the execution when you are four to five steps from the captain or maître d': wet all four fingers of your right hand by running them across your tongue. Quickly rub your wet fingers across your forehead. Now take your left hand (the one with the money) and slap the bill against your forehead. The bill should stick to your forehead (try to make sure the President's face is showing). If your timing is good, you will have arrived within reading distance of the captain just as your left hand falls to your side. *Note:* Do not use this approach with anything under $20; you will look foolish, and the captain/maître d' may refuse to remove the bill from your head. Check the picture below for the correct technique.

WAITERS

The tipping of waiters for service performed—taking your order and delivering it to your table—is easy to handle: leave fifteen percent of the total of the bill (see computation methods in this section), and you won't get hit in the back of the head by a flying plate as you leave.

But, as the angles and planes of proper tipping procedures become more obtuse and wavy, it is best to be aware of the vagaries of the situation, rules to follow, and pitfalls to avoid.

The Presentation of the Check

In better-class restaurants, the check will be delivered to your table on a plastic tray or in a walletlike folder. This *méthode d'emploie* lends a certain amount of dignity to the paying of the bill. You will note that the check will always be facedown. The reason for this is to avoid "check shock." You will be given an appropriate amount of time (considerably shortened if your table is needed) to arrange your cash or credit card. If you are dealing with the walletlike folder, have the cash or credit card peeking out of the top edge. This will avoid the problem of the hovering waiter.

In lesser-class restaurants the random delivery method is used. Your check will be dropped on your table with no regard for its position. Or quick addition may be done at your table while the waiter delivers the ubiquitous parting line: "Will there be anything else?" And there's my favorite: "Pay the cashier when you're ready, hon!" *Note:* If you use a credit card, the charge slip will be paperclipped to the check. You will be asked to sign the charge slip and the check. This verifies that you and the name on the credit card are one and the same, and it also means that you have verified that the total on the charge slip and the check is accurate. Which leads to . . .

The Verification of the Check

Always take the time to check the check.

- Make sure it is, in fact, your check and not that of the high-roller and his niece at the next table.
- Check the addition. Most restaurants employ the "plus one" method—two and two is five, four and four is nine, and so forth.
- Query the waiter. "You charged me for three appetizers, and you will note there are only two of us at the table!" "The wine list price for our wine was $16, you charged me $26!"
- If necessary, go over the check item by item with the waiter. He won't like it, but you will, when you see how much you have saved.

The organization called ERROR (Every Restaurant Rips Off Rubes) has estimated that the overcharge on restaurant checks amounts to approximately $210 million annually. A bill now in Congress (CLC-726) will enable you to take five percent off your entertainment expense as a deductible loss to compensate for restaurant overcharges—if it passes.

The Wrap-Up

As previously stated, leaving fifteen percent of the check is standard tipping practice. But wait! What about the tax? "Don't tip on the tax" is my motto. Follow this example any you will see that doing so could lead to financial ruin.

Total Bill	$82.00	
Tax	5.74	15% on $82.00 is $12.30
Total	$87.74	15% on $87.74 is $13.16

You save $.86 by not tipping on the tax.

Quite obviously, it will take a real cherry picker of a person to leave a $13.16 tip. Most people will round it up to an even $14. You will then have parted with $1.70 more than necessary. Expense account be damned! We're talking real money here!

If, for good reason (bad service, sloppy service, no service, spilled food, blatant addition errors), you leave a tip of less than fifteen percent, or none at all, be prepared to deal with these questions and comments from the captain, waiter, busboy, bread boy, or floor sweeper:

"Was there something wrong with the food?"

"Was there something wrong with the service?"

"You forgot to add in the tip!"

Or, be prepared for the stronger, flat-side-of-the-cleaver approach:

"What's the problem with the tip, Mac?"

"You can tell a cheapo by his shoes!"

"I have been instructed to inform you that this table will be bronzed and never used again in honor of the big spender who just finished eating there!"

Or, beware the it's-an-honest-mistake approach:

"I think you added wrong." (It's really multiplication, but they always say "added.")

"Signore, you left only a tip of 30,000 Lira; I am sure you meant it to be 300,000. You see, 30,000 Lira is only $2.50 in your country—an honest mistake, I'm sure."

Tipping abroad will not be discussed here as fifteen percent is automatically added to the check for parties of zero or more. Don't debate or argue the point. Don't question the arithmetic, either. Why do you think our balance of payments is so out of whack?

Some restaurants have

taken a straightforward approach to the tipping problem. I would like to pass on some recent innovations I have seen.

- *Tipping Chart.* Placed on the table, and similar to the sales tax table used in retail stores, this helps the diner easily determine the amount of the tip. The columns show the amount of the check and the amount to tip at fifteen-, twenty-, and twenty-five-percent rates. Personally, I feel this takes a lot of the fun out of dining out.
- *Tip Chips.* This is the newest wrinkle in the art of tipping. When you enter the restaurant you are asked to estimate what your total tab will be. Let's assume it to be $60. You must then buy, in various denominations, $9 (fifteen percent of the estimated tab total) worth of tip chips. As the drinks, food, and so forth are delivered you can flip a chip to the waiter (if you choose to) for service rendered. Chips left over at the end of the meal are redeemable at the door (if you have a steel spine). Tip chips are not legal tender with the "front people"—captains/maîtres d' get cash only.
- *Scrap Paper.* Pieces of scrap paper are conveniently located between the salt and pepper shakers or the bud vase and the sugar-cube holder. The caption across the top reads "for our doodling friends." The subliminal message is "this will help you figure a nice tip."

MISCELLANEOUS TIPPING

Piano Player at Piano Bar

There will be a brandy snifter or a punch bowl on the piano. The custom is to stuff matching bills into that receptacle (there is always some soft money in it to start), especially if you request a song or sing along. It is not nice to retrieve the money from the glass when the piano player takes a break.

Coat Check

It used to be called *hat check*, but you don't see many hats these days. This is a very seasonal (and regional) factor. Not many coats are checked in California or Florida at any time of the year. And it's a short season for coat checkers in the East and Midwest. The common practice is to hit you with a flat-rate charge. The going rate seems to be $1.50. This conveniently dictates that you should leave $2.00. It is considered cruel and abusive to ask the coat room person to make change. Coat checkers employ the same tactic as piano players—a glass stuffed with paper money—a veritable beacon to attract your money. Even in better-class spots it is expected that you reward the person who found your coat. My compensation package is this: if they give me the coat I came in with, $1.00; if they give me a different coat, $2.00.

Checking expensive fur coats in any restaurant—regardless of the type of restaurant—is akin to playing Russian Roulette with a double-barreled shotgun—you lose fifty percent of the time.

Bartender

If you are prone to frequent a certain bar, you are probably doing the right thing about tipping or you wouldn't be going there regularly.*

Most bartenders are a bit neurotic about receiving only ten percent of the check as a tip when they know that waiters are getting fifteen percent. The theory that waiters work harder and have to put up with progressive aggravation is pure bunk! A waiter, for example, doesn't have to know how to make a Flying Squirrel or a Carmen Miranda drink. Consider, also, that a waiter doesn't have the means to spill a little extra food on your plate like a bartender spills a little extra booze into your glass.

Did you ever have a waiter buy you a free entrée? I say that the bartender dispenses the grease that makes a restaurant run smoothly.

A good bartender is worth a fifteen percent tip, and twenty percent is not out of the question in my book!

Strolling Guitar(s)

This is not an accepted practice in a Real Gourmet Restaurant. However, should you run into a band of these "poblanos," the best way to handle the situation is to ignore them completely. If you request a song, be prepared to pass some pesos to the players. (How you get rid of them after that is your problem.)

*For the record, Real Gourmet Restaurants don't usually have a sit-down bar (stools, etc.). This is done purposely to discourage loud and heavy drinkers.

Espresso Dinero Co.

42117689476329897629654
478503598241

CHEZ VOILA TOUT
Los Angeles, CA

Signature

Name of your bank

Three credit references

Type of Service	Amount
Food	$
Drink	$
Captain's Tip	$
Wine Steward's Tip	$
Waiter's Tip	$
Busboy's Tip	$
Bread Boy's Tip	$
Cloakroom Att. Tip	$
Car Jockey Tip	$
Peter's Pence	$
Presidential Candidate's Fund	$
Subtotal	$
Tax	$
Grand Total	$

Thank you

Here is a sample of a credit card slip. Unless you are paying by cash, or you are a restaurant reviewer, this type of slip will be presented after the meal. You may wish to become acquainted with the format.

Washroom Attendant

The amount of tip is relative to services performed. Here are some guidelines:

Men

Turns on the water and hands you a towel	$ .25
For clothes brushing, *add*	$ .25
For skin bracer, *add*	$ .25
A hot phone number	$5.00
Shoe shine	$1.00

Women

Same as men, *except*

Pressing a dress	$1.00
Removing a stain	$1.00
Blow dry	$2.00

The gourmets, if they are not seated comfortably, and have no elbow room, count both the food and wines for nothing.

Lucien Tendret

11

RESTAURANT CRITICS

The validity of the title of this chapter is somewhat in question. I had toyed with titles like *food evaluators*, *restaurant-reporters*, even *food-appraisers.* It is hard to hang a title on people who write about restaurants because I am not quite sure what it is that they actually do, what they are trying to accomplish, and for whom.

For example, do restaurant critics report on the whole restaurant or just the food? Do (or should) restaurant critics examine the walls, floors, artwork (or lack of same), china, glassware? Or do they not bother with any of these factors and concentrate solely on the service and the food?

Is there a link between bad food and bad walls? Does worn carpeting suggest used or tired food? Does a lack of works of art on the walls mean a lack of creativity in the kitchen? Do plastic flowers in plastic bud vases suggest second-rate buying habits of the management-owners-chef-investors cartel-consortium?

Critic: critical, able to discern; person who indulges in faultfinding and censure.

The key words in the definition are *able to discern, faultfinding,* and *censure.* The synonym for *discern* is *perceive. Perceive* implies keen understanding and insight. I have yet to meet a restaurant critic who has amassed enough knowledge about food, or has been gifted with such extraordinary taste buds that he or she should be bestowed with the title of restaurant (or food) critic. In fact, at this time, there is not a single restaurant or food critic who has even cooked in a restaurant kitchen or one who can cook a meal that borders on palatability, for that matter. The fact that they *think* they can cook doesn't count. One food critic has been making a handsome living by making subtle alterations of recipes from cookbooks and printing them as originals. Then, too, there is some question about the similarity of his taste buds to those of an anteater.

Let's examine the subject in more detail. There are those who postulate that taste buds are vestigal, that unless used they shrivel up and become not unlike wilted celery. Bunk! Taste buds are equal in all people. We are all born with the same number, size, and quality of buds. They don't improve with age or eating, and they don't degenerate if they are not used on a regular basis. There are some who hold that the reverse is true—that if the buds are not overused they become sharper. Consider too, that age does not increase the acuity of taste buds. The reason that babies spit out food is that their taste buds tell them that the food is terrible.

Look into the mouth of a food critic and you will see the same taste buds that you will see when looking in a mirror at your own tongue.

Ludwig Hermansee, professor of *palatology* at the University of Vienna, did a comprehensive study of the taste buds. Over the course of many years he took taste bud samplings from the mouths of food critics from around the world and from regular eaters like you and me. His intensive testing included the use of placebos, bombarding the buds with isotopes and isotopes with the buds, subjection of the buds to cuisines (some *haute* and some not so *haute)*, exposure of the buds to canned, packaged, convenience, franchised, fast, and even British food. The test results were dramatic and conclusive—all taste buds are the same. The so-called "educated" taste buds of the food critics did not respond any differently from those of the "noneducated." The moral here is: "Don't believe everything you read, only what you eat; or, believe what you eat, not what you read."

There are two types of people who report on food and restaurants—*critics* and *reviewers*. Let's identify the major characteristics of the two:

Critics wear disguises and go to restaurants unannounced.
Reviewers make sure that the chef/owner knows they are in the restaurant.

Critics love to find things wrong with a restaurant—from the front door to the kitchen door and everything in between.
Reviewers report on what they ate and how much it cost; as a rule, they don't say too many bad things about the food or the place (otherwise they'll catch hell from the advertising director).

Critics love to send shudders through the owner and put shutters on the windows.
Reviewers love to use those glowing words that pave the way for the people from the advertising department.

Critics are paid a salary that is way too high for what they do.
Reviewers are paid a fixed fee for each restaurant they write up, so they go for speed and volume.

Critics think that reviewers are on the take.
Reviewers feel that critics are snobs.

Reviewers are fatter than critics (remember, more volume).
Critics wear better clothes (they're paid more).

Female critics wear big hats with floppy brims, bad wigs, and sun glasses.

Male critics usually have beards and wear sports coats and penny loafers.

Critics talk into a small microphone that is nestled in a purse or wired down a sleeve.

Reviewers take prodigious notes or talk into a tape recorder while sitting with the owner/chef.

Critics make a reservation under an assumed name (some are rather funny—the name, that is).

Reviewers use their own name (that helps them get a table, more food, service, etc., the next time).

Critics settle the bill with cash.

Reviewers use cash or a credit card (should the owner be stupid enough to present a bill, that is).

Critics use words like *inedible, poorly presented, improper seasoning, salty, rotten service, loud music, oversauced, preprandial.*

Reviewers use superlatives like *flawless, well-balanced, velvety, fork-tender, smooth, napped, understated, Murray from the advertising department will call you next week.*

Restaurant owners and owner chefs take note: Here are two representative drawings (taken from actual file photos) of the male and female species known as *ristorante criticumus.* Post these pictures in your kitchen and make wallet-sized photos for maître d' and captain.

MEN

SIDE VIEW

FRONT VIEW

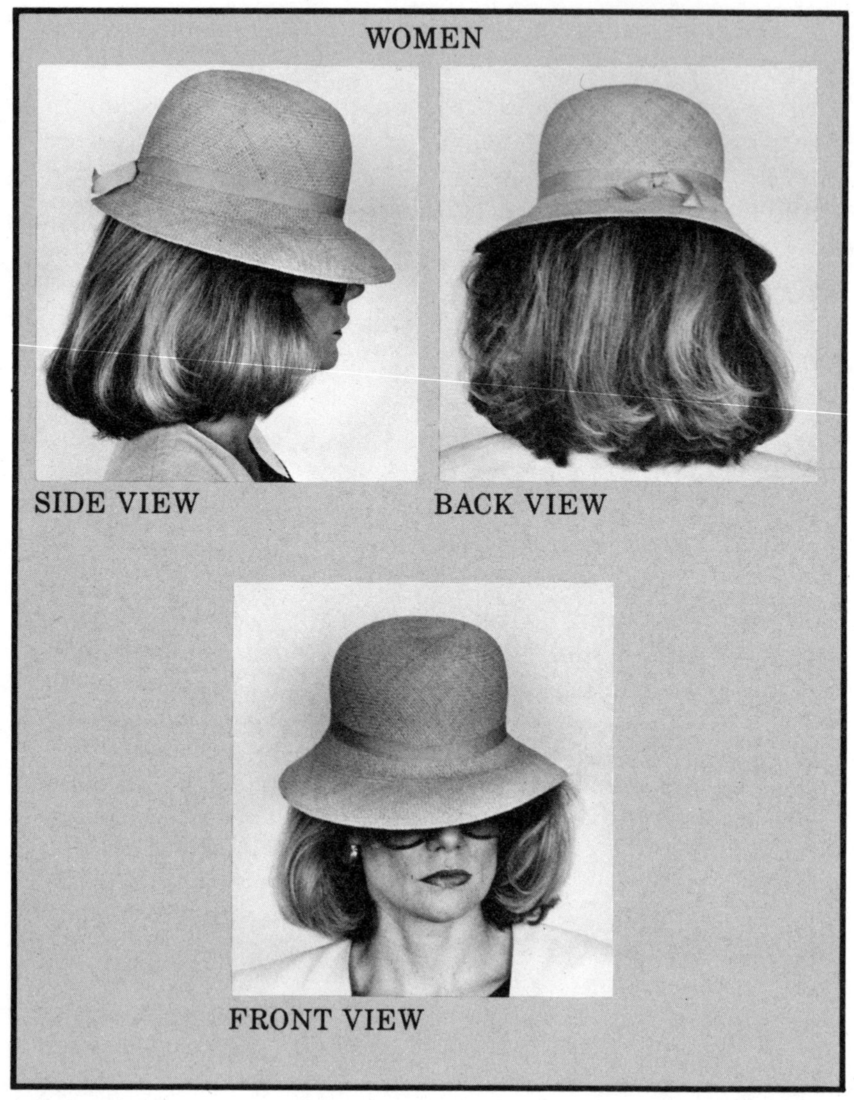
WOMEN
SIDE VIEW
BACK VIEW
FRONT VIEW

How can one criticize a restaurant that has a 32-page menu?

Pierre Pierre

12

THE 1983 SHELLMOBILE DINING AWARDS

Throughout the year food critics employed by a large corporation visit all the restaurants in America. These critics then convene in the city of Plywood, near Minneapolis, to select by secret ballot the top ten restaurants in the country.

The ten selected are the *crème de la crème* and offer the best in food, ambience, service, novelty, creativity, and good taste. It is a high honor in the world of restaurantdom to be selected, and restaurant owners and chefs await with nervous anticipation the final picks of the critics.

The ten terrific are listed on the pages to follow. What, you may ask, do the critics look for? How do they pick the ten terrific and by what method?

An unnamed source has managed to provide us with one of the secret ballots used by the critics for the awarding of points. It is reprinted here for your edification and so that you can become an armchair restaurant critic.

The name of the restaurant on the critique sheet has been blanked out as a matter of courtesy.

TOP SECRET TOP SECRET TOP SECRET

1983 SHELLMOBILE SCORING SHEET

Restaurant Name:

Points to be awarded for:	*# of possible points*	*Actual*
Being able to find the restaurant	8	
Architectural interest	3	
Chef-owned	8	
Greek-owned	10	
Menus	6	
Menu selection	3	
Creativity of menu	4	
Free parking	10	
Telephone reservations taken	9	
Has strict dress code	2	
Flocked wallpaper	7	
Fountain in the foyer	8	
Table covering		
a) paper	6	
b) oilcloth	6	
c) cloth	6	
d) none	6	
Napkins		
a) paper	8	
b) cloth	8	
Dishes		
a) matched	7	
b) mismatched	6.5	
Glassware		
(same as dishes)		
Waiters' (or waitresses') outfits		
a) theme costume	7	
b) casual	7	
c) formal	4	
d) random	6	
Flowers		
a) artificial	5	
b) real	5	
c) none	7	
Service		
a) some	3	
b) little	4	
c) none	3	
d) expert	5	

Critic's Name:		
Location:	**Date Visited:**	
Points to be awarded for:	*# of possible points*	*Actual*
Cooking is done		
a) in kitchen	6	
b) tableside	2	
c) outside	3	
ADDED ATTRACTIONS		
Lingerie fashion show	10	
Electronic games	8	
Piano bar	3	
Piano bar with piano player	1	
Harpist	3	
Stage show	5	
Strolling guitarist	0	
Owner who sings	1	
Waiters (or waitresses) who sing	0	
If above are in college, deduct	-6	
Jukebox	7	
Movies	5	
OTHER		
Maître d'	7	
Maîtresse d'	8	
No d'	9	
RESTAURANT IS:		
Rotating	2	
Nonrotating	8	
At street level	7	
Above street level	4	
Below street level	9	
ARTWORK		
Some	7	
None	7	
Real	7.5	
Modern	7.75	
Naked ladies	10	
BAR IS:		
Sit-down	9	
Stand-up	7.5	
None	1	
Cute	0	

THE SHELLMOBILE TEN TERRIFIC FOR 1983

THE SQUID HOUSE
452 Deveraux
Savannah, Georgia
Seafood

Uninvitingly grubby, backyard-type spot near some water that would throw you off at first, but the squid is outstanding. It's fixed at least twenty-three ways; if you're a squid lover, this place is for you. For openers, try the squid appetizer: the squid is ringed onto a sesame bread stick and stuck upright in a zippy-dippy-peppery red sauce. One of the main-course main attractions is squid *sur la table:* fresh squid is brought tableside for personal selection and then, to the diner's delight, is killed, cleaned, cut, and cooked at table. How it's cooked is a your-choice affair—deep-fried (watch out for the spattering grease), boiled, sautéed, or flambéed. Prices for this entrée are by the pound (before cooking). For dessert, don't miss squid *à la* Jello: choice of six fruit flavors that jiggle enticingly around brandy-soaked squid ringlets. Limited wine list. Root beer by the pitcher. Service is charmingly inept. Lunch 11:00 A.M.–2:00 P.M. Dinner 5:00–10:00 P.M. 652-1186.

LE GROSFRANC
Regency Towers
Houston, Texas
Nouvelle Avant-Garde

A *tour de force* restaurant that serves cracking-good meals. The prices are steep, but the food is so heavenly that it levitates off the plate, so it really doesn't hurt when it comes time to unhinge the old wallet. The ambience is strictly *à la Française:* pictures of the great chefs of France, from Brillat-Savarin to Freddy Cacher, are interspersed with bright *fleur de lis en neon.* The miniature Eiffel Tower–shaped candle centerpieces add to the panache. Chef Banque-Franc, the creator of Nouvelle Avant-Garde cuisine (it's fresh, refined, simple, light, willowy, far-reaching, tamed, clever, and packs gustatory wallop), is not afraid to delve into the unknown, a trait that is hard to find in restaurants today. Two of the dishes that exemplify the lusty savor of Chef Banque-Franc's cooking are Blanquette de Langoustines et de Turbot aux Artichauts, Champignons, Macre ou Chataigne d'Eau, Piments Doux, Olives Noir, Oignons, et de Garni de Persil; and Omelette Fourrée aux Pommes Dite à la Normande à la Mousse Chantilly en Croute. Both dishes are the ultimate distillation of simplicity and are worth trying. The dishes are numbered on the menu (à la Chinois) to speed up ordering and to peel away any trepidation about pronouncing the words correctly. Lunch noon–3:00 P.M. Dinner 7:00–10:30 P.M. 777-1444. ① ② ③ $$$

CHARLES
112 Polk Street
San Francisco, California
Mixed

My first report was not encouraging: Charles, the owner, knew something was amiss when I asked for "a little off the sides and a shoe shine." This blew my cover (all my restaurant visits are anonymous). The fact is that this restaurant is really a hairdressing salon (or is it a hairdressing salon that is a restaurant?).

The decor is a real whistler: subtle orchestrations of vibrant colors are punctuated by walls, floors, and ceilings, the whole of which is set off here and there by mural vignettes of capering monkeys.

Meals are served *en dryer* and are some of the best of the genre. Top choices from soup to dessert are: Snip Soup—clear rabbit broth topped with snipped chives; Roller Salad—lettuce leaves rolled around chopped lamb balls; Bleached Veal Cosmos—pale fork-tender veal, gently bedded in an ethereally light spinach sauce. A selection of seasonal fruits gently bathed in simple syrup round out the menu.

Service flags under the strain of the restaurant's dual personality (the coutures also serve the food). It's a fun place if Charles is in a good mood. It's a lousy place to get a crew cut. Reservations are a must. Call for a booking as hours do vary.

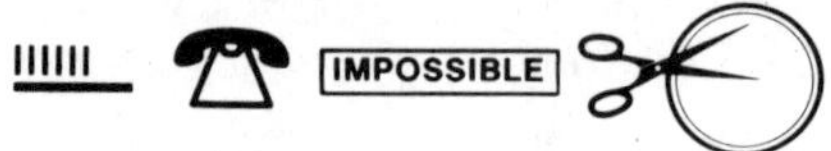

VEGGIE JACKSON'S
12 Sea Bay Road
Long Beach, California
Vegetarian

This dining spa is a veritable garden of delights. Diners are seated around the perimeter of a one-acre living and growing garden, the whole of it being neatly glassed in. *Fresh* is the mode word here. No menus are proffered as one can select dishes directly from the vegetable-laden pushcarts that are rolled tableside. Better still is an adventuresome trip directly to the seventy-two-item salad garden. Crops are rotated, and no insecticides are used. Entrées include lettuce ($1.85 a head), eggplant ($1.50 each), tomatoes ($1.89 a pound), celery ($1.29 a bunch), cucumbers ($.50 each). A real standout is Avocados Bert: spiked with natural protein and aged for three months in natural fertilizer, the taste is indescribable. Desserts include Carrots Flambé, Radish Soufflé, and green peppers stuffed with crushed macaroons and napped with a *zabaglione* sauce. Lunches are fun, as you get to watch the field workers hoe and irrigate the crops. Avoid the inside tables as they tend to get wet from the sprinkler system. Lunch 11:00 A.M.–2:00 P.M. Dinner 5:00–9:30 P.M. 842-2194. YES

CHEZ ROCCO
11 Lago Way
Beverly Hills, California
Italo-French

An onrushing wave in the heavy sea of cuisine, this toney spa has been dubbed "the stomach to the stars." Combining the best in food from two countries, it doesn't let its name down. Busts of the great chefs of France and one from Italy line the pink shagged wall entryway. The twelve-seat dining room (with retractable ceiling) is a *trompe l'oeil,* as is the food: served on mirror-lined plates so patrons can see themselves and what they are eating brings confidence and credibility back into eating. Recommendations for starters: Écrevisse Stuffed with Prosciutto, Fried Eggplant *en Sac,* and Italian Sausage Stuffed with Truffles. Entrées run the gamut from Linguini-Stuffed Sole to crab stuffed with ricotta cheese that's stuffed into smoked salmon and dusted with a fine spray of Parmesan cheese—a formidable dish. Don't let the Chariot Le Dolce pass you by as the desserts are good. The French side of the chariot offers fifteen hot and cold soufflés, twenty-six assorted tarts, bombes, flambés, and sorbets; the Italian side offers a nice selection of apples and pears. Service is a bit schizoid, as is the wine selection. Both of the chefs are ambidextrous, which makes for a smoother-running kitchen, but the *éminence grise* that makes this place tick is Sonny Battuta, a native of Calamari del Mare and former shoe salesman to royalty. No lunch. Dinner 9:00 P.M.–2:00 A.M. Late-night supper starts at 3:00 A.M. Luxury car parking only. Reservations *de rigueur.* No ties allowed.

MAYBE

THE EIGHT IMPECCABLES
1242½ Merlot Street
New York City
Chinese

This spot is squeaky-clean and charmingly unassuming; and the decor is inscrutable, but the food is not. There are honest-to-goodness regional dishes from the provinces here: King Kong (dragon whisker soup), Ice Tong (thirty-one flavors chicken), Hung Shoe (stir-fried MSG), and Duck Cow (hooey, looey, dooey pressed duck). In addition, there are rarely seen authentic dishes such as Stuffed Pong Balls, Sub Gum Wrappers, Rin Tin Tin Shrimp, and Sweet and Sour Tongue Depressors. A nice touch is the bowl of artificial waxed rice centerpiece on each table. The ninety-six-page menu does away with the yawn bore of columns A, B, and C but does translate the American into French, German, Italian, Russian, and Irish. A dessert to experience, which is *le specialtie de la maison* (sic): The Eight Impeccables happy smile precious kumquats in a sweet pesto sauce—a real cymbal clanger. The taco shells heaped with fortunes (not a bad one in the bunch) put the finishing touch on a pleasant meal. Wan Fu wine is available by the pitcher. Lunch 10:00 A.M.–2:00 P.M., 10:30 A.M.–1:30 P.M., 11:00 A.M.–1:00 P.M., 11:30 A.M.–12:30 P.M. Dinner follows similar feedings. 765-8422.

INN OF THE HOLIDAYS
1064 Frontage Road
Moultrie, Georgia
Continental

The Venetian dining room at this roadside motel is amuck with waterways and gondolas. And would you believe gondolas are used to take diners to their tables? Every table is set on its own little island, complete with an artificial palm tree. (Obviously, no one told the designer of this place that Venice has no palm trees.) Waiters scuba up tableside, take your order, and disappear back into the water. The food is then delivered by paddleboat. The total effect seems a bit on the wishy-washy side; the food is too. As you may have surmised, seafood is the *tour de force* mainstay of the menu. Appetizers to try: Mock Deviled Crab Eggs, Escargot Stuffed with Crab, Shrimp Stuffed with Anchovy Olives. Entrées follow the Pisces trail, with Dover Sole O Mio (puréed Dover sole in a marinara sauce) leading the way. Another entrée of note: hush puppies stuffed with catfish. Desserts carry on the water theme with Salt Water Taffy Soufflé (sixteen flavors), and Pear Poisson (catch-o-the-day is stuffed into a poached pear and napped with a clam stock reduction). Service can be a bit noisy, as the gondoliers blow their air horns at the waterway intersections; on a busy night the noise level drowns out polite table talk. Lunch 11:00 A.M.–2:00 P.M. Dinner 5:00–9:00 P.M. Sunday brunch 7:00–9:00 A.M. 884-1447.

DEFINITELY

CAFÉ AMBIENCE
428 East State Parkway
Chicago, Illinois
Unknown

Decorated by owner Michael Bruce-Bruce, this place reeks of its name. Plushy two-inch deep carpeting, rosewood walls, *real* Louis XIV chairs, Belgian linens, silver, crystal, brocade, tapestries, fresh flowers, and tailed waiters (costumes by Marcel) are just a few of the ambient amenities. Skip all of the appetizers; they are overpriced and dreadful. Entrées don't fare much better, but if you must eat (the place is the thing here) try the Saddle of Turtle sans Croute. Desserts are the mundane classics and are better left for the kitchen staff to eat. Espresso by the carafe. Good selection of Upper Wisconsin wines. Service is composed and suave. The steadily pounding Bach concertos could drive one up a banana tree for good. Dinner 7:00–9:00 P.M. 463-9078.

MENDEL, MENDEL, AND MENDEL
26 Well Street
New Haven, Connecticut
American

Three brothers, all lawyer dropouts, opened this wood-paneled, plush-carpeted spot shortly after the Joe McCarthy hearings. Diners are asked to sign a no-fault contract prior to eating, should they fall ill from the food and try to sue. The menu is priced by the hour. Appetizers run about $10 (twelve minutes), entrées $40 (twenty-five to twenty-six minutes), and desserts $7 (six to seven minutes). Soufflés can run into big bucks—go for the fresh fruit. Don't dawdle over coffee or afterdinner drinks—you'll need a second mortgage on the summer place (Shelly Mendel is good at second mortgages). Try to avoid lengthy conversations with the brothers Mendel (who are peripatetically nimble of foot). As you may have guessed, service is slow. A few suggestions to keep the tab down: Now Therefore Soup (five minutes), Whereas Chicken (eighteen minutes), Be It Resolved Salad (five minutes), and Tort Tart (four minutes). This should keep the bill to around $50, tax and tip not included. Wine is priced by the case. Deveined ice water is complimentary. Lunch 11:00 A.M.–3:00 P.M. Dinner 5:00–10:00 P.M. 422-7999.

IL BORDELLO
246 West 46th Street
New York City
Nord-Est Italian

This restaurant has a lot of fame—none of which is ill—in spite of its name. Opened just three years ago by the Puttana sisters as a storefront venture, it has become the *alla moda* spot for those who know good *cucina d'Italia.*

Rosie Puttana handles the front, and her sister, Sensualità, is the *capo cuoca.* Sensualità seems to have a knack for spices and herbs, and on balance, she works wonders with basil, oregano, and red pepper. Noteworthy dishes are Camera da Letto Veal and Spaghetti Puttanesca. (It is said that this dish originated in the Puttana family many years ago, and the Puttana family lawyer, Sano Rubizzo, has lawsuits pending against all restaurants that serve this "family name" dish. Mr. Rubizzo says, "Let them serve it all they want, but my client deserves a royalty for every dish of Spaghetti Puttanesca served in the United States and maybe even Italy.")

A dessert of note is Whipped Zabaglione with Fresh Cherries. There is an excellent selection of Calabrian wines. The reflocked wallpaper, dim lighting, and pinky-ring piano player add immensely to the non-prima donna aura.

Private dining rooms for two are available on the second floor. Reservations *mandatore.* No lunch. Dinner 5:00 P.M.–4:00 A.M. 234-4234. Open every day.

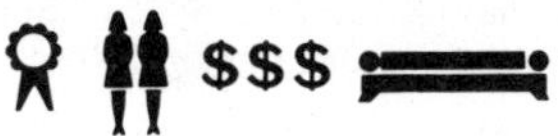

13

CUISINE COMIQUE

It is only *par chance* that *The Official Gourmet Handbook* is able to bring to you the startling information that follows: Some time ago we placed a mole in a well-known, two-star restaurant just outside of Paris. We had heard that its chef/owner was on to something really big, and we wanted to be ready when that culinary big-bang happened. Well, the bang happened; and, fortunately, our mole was able to take a few pictures (on the pages that follow) by using a hidden camera. These pictures are representative of a new and startling—almost revolutionary—approach to *haute cuisine.*

Brilliant in its inception and magnificent in its presentation, this is truly the work of a genius. It is certain that the third star for (restaurant unnamed) is just over the horizon.

We have also learned through our mole that Chef (unnamed) is calling his exciting new culinary creations *cuisine comique.* Oh, yes! This is the stuff that makes the blood course violently through the veins of the Real Gourmet.

Note: We would like to thank Olivia de Pitts, former restaurant critic, now third executive chef to the premier of France, for her help in finding and placing the mole.

Cinq Petits Radis Dans un Bateau en Concombre (five little radishes in a cucumber boat).

Un Jeune Homme Radis Dans un Bateau—une Mer de Sauce (a young radish boy in a boat on a sea of sauce).

Avocat et Patate avec Poivrons Douces (avocado and potato with sweet peppers).

Jeune Fille de Poivrons et de Macaroni (young lady made with peppers and macaroni).

Nouilles en Forme d'Alphabet—Sauce Italien (alphabet noodles in tomato sauce).

Seins de Melon avec des Cerises dans une Sauce Pâteuse (breast of melon with cherries in a soft sauce).

Un Jeune Homme Radis Canotage au Coulis de Tomates Parfumé à l'Estragon (a young radish boy boating in tomatoes flavored with tarragon).

Quatre Petits Radis dans l'Auto en Courgette—Sauce Le-Mans (four little radishes in a zucchini auto—Sauce Le-Mans).

Chou Tête avec Chapeau (head of cabbage with hat).

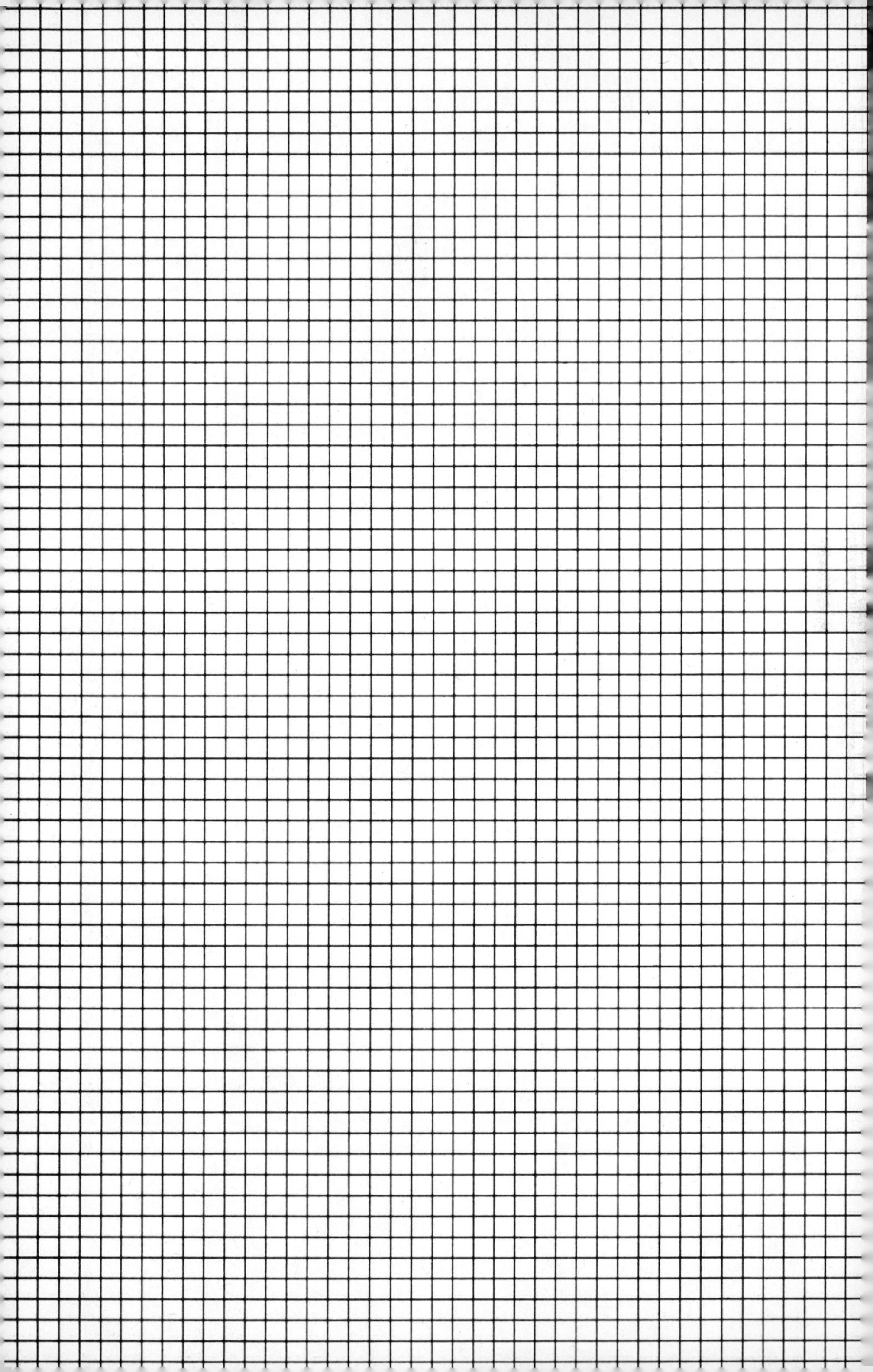

PART III
ENTERTAINING CHEZ VOUS

In Parts I and II you learned many things that will help you master your Gs (Gourmet, Gourmand, and Gastronome). We now begin Part III. Part III deals generally with situations found outside of the restaurant environment and inside your own dining room—party planning, dinner conversation, recipes, dress codes, food facts. This is the stage of fine tuning, when you master the details that on the surface may seem trivial but in fact are heavy with significance to the Real Gourmet.

Real Gourmets know the sometimes unbearable weight that they shoulder. They are called on, time and again, by friends and relatives for advice on restaurants, cooking, recipes, protocol—every type of information connected with dining and drinking. If you are fortunate enough (and a lot of money doesn't necessarily make it any easier) to achieve Real Gourmet status, be prepared to bear the burden that goes with the distinction.

Read on and reach out for those three stars. One day, you too may be able to master your Gs and then go on to help others master theirs.

The same intelligence is required to marshall an army in battle as to have a good party. The first must be as formidable as possible, the second as pleasant as possible.

Aemilus Paulus

14

PARTY PLANNING

It's easy to have a bad time at your own party, but you don't have to, if you follow some basic rules and do some planning. Also, it isn't necessary to push yourself to exhaustion because of last-minute shopping and unnecessary worry over what could go wrong.

The host or hostess who wishes to avoid trauma that a party can unmercifully wreak should use the Party Planning Guide below. Developed by master caterer Felipe Camel-Back, the guide is a digest version of the type that he uses when doing a do for several hundred or more. Mr. Camel-Back is a party pro. His firm, located in San Diego, has catered parties for people who *really* know how to party. Also pay attention to his perfect party tips, and your party will be on the lips of your guests for many months.

PARTY PLANNING GUIDE

This guide assumes a Saturday party. If the party is on a Friday, move everything by one day.

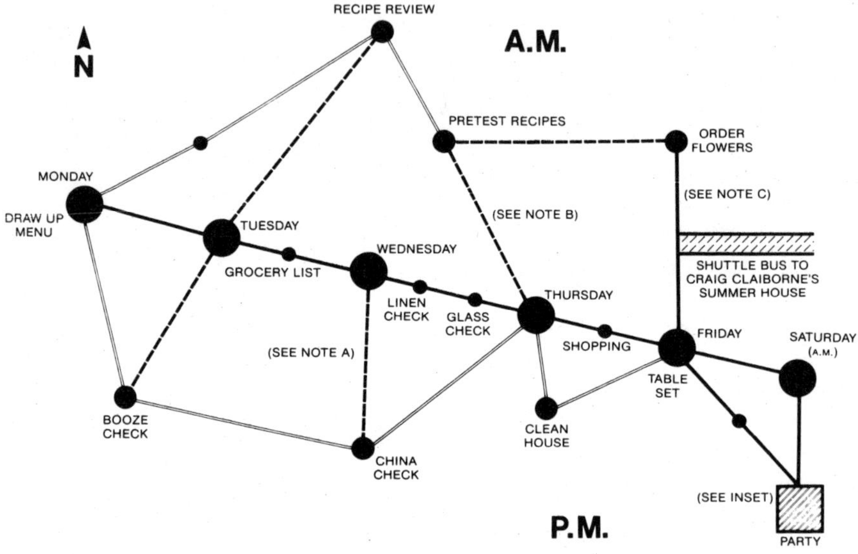

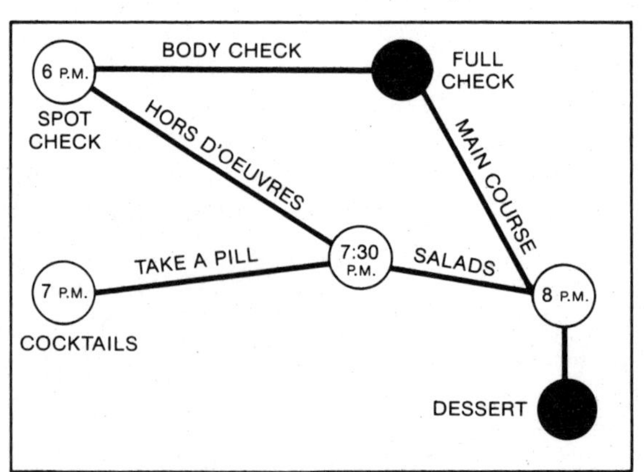

NOTE A
SOUTHBOUND ON ALTERNATE DAYS

NOTE B
NORTHBOUND ON SUNDAY AFTER "60 MINUTES"

NOTE C
CLOSED, CONSTRUCTION IN PROGRESS

To make a splash at the next formal dinner party you attend, take a cue from this well-dressed couple.

FELIPE CAMEL-BACK'S PARTY TIPS

Establish the party theme early. Japanese lanterns are easy to find in San Francisco but hard to come by in Bangor, Maine, so early theme planning is important. Don't let the time of year or the climate affect your choice of theme. For example, if you live in Chicago, you can have a beach party party right in your home or apartment in February; spread sand around the house (white sand works nicely), have beach balls, rubber rafts, beach chairs, and so forth strewn around for your guests' enjoyment. Consider, too, an après ski party in Florida—bring in snow, wear ski clothes, serve hot wine.

Establish the party ambience. Will the guests sit or stand? Will the party be inside or outside? Consider available space for the number of guests invited (the rule of thumb: standing—one guest per square foot; sitting—one guest per three square feet; a combination of both—divide by two).

Send invitations early. This will rule out a negative reply from people who can't stand your parties. Send out the initial invitation at least three months ahead, a follow-up invitation 30 days ahead, a telegram two weeks ahead, and a personal phone call one week ahead. Your invitation should state at least one or more of the following: date, time, place, dress,* occasion, RSVP, regrets only, children, pets, divorced, separated, smoking-nonsmoking, your net worth. If you throw frequent, large parties, get a bulk mailing permit to cut down on the mailing costs. Last, but less than least, the style of your invitations is a personal reflection of your taste, so keep this in mind when purchasing or making your invitations.

China, paper, plastic, paper towels. Decide early what your guests will be eating from. Strict etiquette dictates the following: If the party is between 7:00 A.M. and 1:00 P.M., paper plates are OK for sandwiches, canapes, etc. (exception to this is scrambled eggs or Eggs Benedict—use plastic plates). Between 1:00 P.M. and 4:00 P.M., use plastic or paper plates. After 6:00 P.M. you must use something hard like china, melamine, glass. If using plastic or paper, try to locate some unusual shapes or colors to add interest.

If your party guests will outnumber your china, don't be afraid to rent. Do avoid renting from companies that have their advertising message on the front of the plate rather than on the back.

Don't serve dishes that require last-minute cooking. Cooking at the last minute is nerve-wracking at best. A good idea is to make one spectacular dish yourself (whichever one you are famous for) and get everything else from a reputable gourmet takeout shop. To avoid being a servant at your own party, try a stove buffet—have your guests help themselves

*If an invitation reads "Black Tie," this means a tuxedo for the man and a long gown for the lady. This is an unbreakable rule. If you show up in any other dress mode, you will be shut off from food and drink and shut out of all conversation (see photo).

right out of the pots on your kitchen stove. A do-it-yourself cooking party is also fun—each guest makes his own soufflé, Ballottine de Canard, Scallopini Castelli Romano. You supply the ingredients; your guests do the cooking. This takes a lot of pressure off you.

The cocktail question. An open bar can be financially devastating. Here are some alternatives: serve only cheap jug wine; serve only cheap beer; make a punch; or state on the invitation "Limit two drinks per person."

How much to have on hand is relative to the number of guests and the length, style, type, and latitude of the party. Another thumb rule: Beer—four bottles per male guest, zero bottles per female. Hard liquor—one-half bottle per male guest, one bottle per female. Wine—same as hard liquor, multiplied by two.

Mixers to have on hand: club soda, tonic water, imported and domestic water, cider, Mellow-Yellow, Kitchen Aid.

What about flowers? Flowers are a must, and they should follow the party theme. But, if fresh flowers are not in the budget, substitute vegetables: celery, lettuce, radishes, corn on the cob, artichokes. All can be displayed beautifully in baskets or bowls or arranged artfully around the house. Plastic flowers, fruits, or vegetables are totally unacceptable at any party.

Music must be compatible with the theme. Don't play a Bach concerto at a build-your-own taco party or Earth, Wind, and Fire, at a formal sit-down. If in doubt about your music program, have your music monger put together a program that includes your favorite selections and those of your guests.

Live music adds a touch of class, but you must use good judgment. A harpist at an elegant dinner is rich, but a harmonica player is not. If you are planning to "go live," deal with a reputable talent agency. Many a hostess has been mortified by bumbling, drunken, and talentless musicians. Ask for references and an audition, if in doubt.

The smoking question. One way to solve this sticky problem is to have a place on your invitation for the invitees to check off *smoking* or *nonsmoking.* If it's a sit-down affair, you can reserve one side of the table for smokers and one side for nonsmokers (make sure the ashtrays are on the proper side of the table). If it's a buffet, set up tables in separate rooms and direct your guests accordingly to the smoking or nonsmoking room. Or set aside one room or area of the house for smokers to repair to when they want to light up—bathroom, terrace, back porch, front porch. Cigar and pipe smoking should not be tolerated. Inform your guests of this either on the invitation or over the PA system at the start of the party.

Plan several parties back to back. Better still, plan back-to-back-to-back-to-back parties. This eliminates duplication of work. Cook lots of food for the "back" party, then just reheat the leftovers (or primp them up to look fresh) for the next "back" party, and so forth. This method helps to loosen any social logjams that may have built up on your calender.

Don't be tense at your own party. Your guests will pick up on your mood and your party will turn into a wake. Avoid PT (party tenseness) by popping a few pills or slugging down a couple of drinks about 30 minutes before your guests are due to arrive.

"The success of a party is in direct proportion to the amount of food that is served." That was the philosophy of Lucius Lucinius Lucullus, a noted glutton. Lucullus once spent $90,000 on a dinner party for three people—Pompey, Cicero, and himself. (Eat your scarf off, Craig Claiborne.) If you are having a buffet, heap the tables with mountains of food. If it's a sit-down dinner, go for 10–12 well-endowed courses. "There is no excuse for short rations at any party," says CeCe Back-Bay, a consummate party giver. "I would

rather save up for three to four years and have one grand event than have several parties a month and have them be subgrand."

The lingering guest problem. There are several effective methods for dealing with this situation:

- Cut off all drinks—booze, coffee, water.
- Start to clean up (vacuuming is effective).
- Make an announcement over the PA system that this is the termination of the party.
- Ask pointed questions: "Is my watch right?" "Is it as late as I think it is?" "Did I hear a rooster crow?"
- Excuse yourself, change into bed clothes, and start to turn off the lights.

Seating arrangements. This can be tricky at formal dinner parties.* Follow these rules:

- When the dinners number six, ten, or fourteen the host is seated at one end of the table, the hostess at the other.
- If the guests number eight or twelve and you wish to alternate men and women, put the host at one end and the hostess to the left of the other end.
- For any numbers not covered above, random seating is acceptable.
- If the honor guest is a woman, she is seated to the right of the host; if a man, to the left of the hostess.
- If the honor guest or guests cannot be readily determined, a secret ballot may be necessary to select an honor guest or two, or ask for volunteers.

---

*Mr. Camel-Back adds a side-note here concerning seating arrangements in restaurants. He jokingly refers to guests milling around the table and deciding who sits next to whom as the "Danse d'Oiseaux Mangeant" (rough translation: Dance of the Eating Birds).

His advice on how to avoid this type of seating confusion: Assign a number—1, 2, 3, etc.—to each seat around the table. Then write the names of the eaters on little slips of paper. Have the restaurant captain draw names. The first name he calls gets seat number one, the second name gets seat number two, and so forth.

Felipe's Dinner Etiquette[1]

- It goes without saying that food is always served from the *left* side of the guest (and passed that way, too).
- Wine is *always* poured into the glass from the *right* side.
- Plates are always removed from the *right.*
- After the salad course, the table is denuded and crumbed.[2]
- Finger bowls should be placed on a doily that has been placed on a fruit plate .
- Cream and sugar should be passed together on a small tray; otherwise one or the other will get lost in the shuffle. Then you have to ask and answer a lot of questions: "Have you had the cream?" "No, I haven't had the sugar."
- A formal dinner requires that there be some type of service help. A dinner cannot really be called formal if the host and hostess are carrying and serving the food. Good places to find service help are the local Boy Scout troop and senior citizens' homes.

---

1. For more detailed information on etiquette and manners, refer to Mr. Camel-Back's nifty book, C.R.U.D.E. (Complete, Responsible, and Usable Dinner Etiquette).
2. A small hand-held, battery-operated vacuum cleaner works nicely.

Enchant, stay beautiful and gracious; but to do this, eat well. Bring the same consideration to the preparation of your food as you devote to your appearance. Let your dinner be a poem, like your dress.

Monselet
Lettres à Emilie

15

ARE YOU WHAT YOU WEAR?

What to wear? What to wear? Three simple words that plague every hostess when it's party time. The problem may seem trite to those who normally use a caterer, but to the woman who is a serious cook, the woman who puts her all into a party or dinner, the woman who does not compromise in the planning or precision of her affair, the question of dress can be as formidable as the food she hopes to serve. If you classify yourself as a hostess, and a bona fide cook, don't be afraid to wear an apron throughout the party; it must be a serious apron—oversized, sturdy, no frills. This look will lend a lot of credibility to your food. If, on the other hand, you hate aprons, there are solutions: clean, oversized T-shirts, cotton jumpsuits, men's pajama tops.

There is little doubt that most hostesses will totally reject the idea of wearing anything except their very best—heavy cooking stains, and odors aside. After all, successful parties are a total-effect situation: food, fun, and fashion.

Food and fashion should not be in competition with each other—that's a basic rule. If you are planning to show off a new designer fashion, the food should play a secondary role and not upstage your outfit. Conversely, if you plan to wear something simple, then the food should assume the missionary position. Don't, for example, put your newest St. Laurent in competition with a spectacular display of hors d'oeuvres; neither will have been served justly.

Another example: Let's say that you are having a build-your-own-sandwich buffet; by all means, dress to both ears with the finest your closet has to offer. You will be, and as hostess rightfully so, the center of attention.

An easy way out for any occasion is to wear "something picked up in Tangiers." A brightly splashed caftan or djellaba works nicely, but don't forget the color rules: if serving lobster, don't wear red; serving shrimp, avoid pink. "Don't clash with your food" is an old party axiom.

Now, about perfume. Your perfume should not overpower your food, nor should your food overpower your perfume. Good balance and an understanding of odors are strong considerations. For example, garlicky dishes may call for something from your *batterie de parfums* that is on the heavy side. Aromatic dishes, like Coq au Vin, would dictate that you wear something light. Costume mode is directly related to party ambience: location, size of room, ventilation. Will the party or dinner be on the patio, in the kitchen, in your van? Who's doing the cooking, the cleaning up, the serving? All factors must be considered and your clothes selected accordingly.

Here are some dress tips for the hostess:

- Wool and chili are natural enemies—one must go when the other is present.
- Gold bracelets conduct heat; paste jewelery will melt.
- Have several scarves handy to cover up the spots that will show up on your outfit just when you least expect them.
- Cook everything several days ahead and reheat everything at the last minute.
- Don't taste anything while wearing lipstick; everything will be cherry flavored.
- Don't wear a blouse or dress with free-flowing sleeves if you plan to flambé—*you* may become an unplanned entrée or dessert.
- Wear bright colors if the party is upbeat, subdued colors if the party is downbeat.

Let us now discuss the dress code for suburban patio parties. The rule is: there are no rules. The reason for this is that one is faced with constantly changing conditions—climatic and others. If you dress lightly, you'll be fine until the sun goes down; then you will freeze. If you dress too heavily, you'll sweat off six pounds until the sun sinks. If you wear your most expensive perfume, it will be wiped out in ten seconds by the smoke from the charcoal grill. If you insist on wearing white, then you and the redwood furniture deserve each other. (Redwood furniture is your dry cleaner's favorite type of outdoor furniture.)

Rain, wind, sun, smog, insects, smoke, grass, sticky-fingered kids, dirty-pawed dogs, dirt, dust—there's just too much to deal with at outdoor parties. My advice is good advice; don't have outdoor parties. You'll be a much nicer person in the long run. Don't have them, even if your husband or friend volunteers to do all the work. They have no control over the elements, the smoke, the kids.

TIPS FROM HOSTS WITH THE MOST

Once again, we went to our *Dinner Party Who's Who* book and contacted some of the most knowledgeable party flingers for their comments. Here is what they have to say:

Marina del Rey is the owner of a chic boutique in Beverly Hills and a prima-class party person. "Nothing frilly," she states. "Frilly is for kids. Look seductive, wear revealing clothes. You should be the center of attention, not the food. Never, never," she adds, "wear the same outfit twice. This is a serious *faux pas de fête.*"

Guy Marcel is the fashion consultant to the Great Chefs of France. Guy sees nothing wrong with a hostess donning the traditional chef's garb—chef's jacket, checkered pants, running shoes, and a tall white toque. Guy maintains that if a chef can mingle with the guests in his restaurant with that outfit, then a hostess can do the same at her own party or dinner.

Holly DeLesseps is an interior designer based in Dallas. Holly feels that the hostess should wear a costume in keeping with the type of food being served. "Authentic Italian dress when serving Italian food. A beret is chic when doing it *à la Française,*" he suggests. "Themes are important at any social event," he adds. "And a party without a theme is like a comb without teeth."

Cantwell Porsky, a professional party thrower from New York City, is adamant about casual. Running shoes, baggy polo khakis, and an oversized Izod shirt is the choice of Mr. Porsky. "There is no excuse for being uncomfortable at your own do," says Mr. Porsky. "I don't care if I look like a multicolored doormat. My food is my statement," he adds.

Doris Butts is a real estate developer from Chicago. Doris suggests building a dressing room just off the kitchen. "It's the ultimate answer," she states. "I have my change of clothes ready to go, put the final touch on the Jell-O punch, and dash into the dressing room. I am at my very best when the butler opens the door to greet the first guest."

Good food and a beautiful table are dandy,
But a foot in the mouth comes in handy.
Mindy Peltwell

16

THE FINE ART OF DINNER CONVERSATION

Mindy Peltwell, who entertains frequently and formally in her Hamptons beach house, her Carolina hunt house, her villa on the Costa del Molé, and her New York apartment, was gracious enough to share her ideas on how to light the conversational flame that sets a party aglow. Mindy's premise that "good talk can make bad food taste like ambrosia" is solid advice. Here are some of Mindy's tips on the fine art of dinner talk.

CONVERSATION AVANT-DINNER (OR PREPRANDIAL PATTER)

The most tense moment for every host or hostess is that time between the arrival of the last guest and the sitting down to dinner. Introductions have been made, drinks offered, and hors d'oeuvres proffered.

What do you do if the conversation is not building at an acceptable rate? What do you do if the guests are sitting around like lumps on the sofa, staring into space?

It may be too late to do anything at this point, and your fête may fall like a badly made soufflé. You must do "conversational planning," much like you do menu planning.

"Conversation does not always expand to fill the void that silence creates" is an axiom that should be committed to memory. Another good axiom to remember is "silence is anesthesia." What can the novice party-thrower do to get pre-dinner conversation off to a fast start? Here is some advice that should help.

- The afternoon of the party, remove all the furniture in the house. It is a known fact that sitting people talk less than standing people.
- Serve only hard liquor: double vodkas, stiff martinis, and straight gin get those tongues moving a lot faster than white wine.
- If you have pets—dogs, cats, birds—have them around. Pets invite inane yet entertaining tales of what they eat, funny things they do, how they were named, and so forth.
- Invite a colorful relative that you can count on to talk loudly, tell foul jokes, and insult several guests.
- Serve interesting hors d'oeuvres[1]—cocktail franks Wellington, chestnuts wrapped in bologna slices, mock shrimp balls, truffle-flavored popcorn, duck wings, anchovies stuffed with olives, and things like that. Interesting hors d'oeuvres always generate interesting conversation.
- If it is a large party, say thirty or more guests, issue name tags at the door. The tag should state the bearer's occupation and gross income. This makes it easy for people with similar interests, and at the same social level, to cling together—lawyers will mingle with lawyers, doctors with doctors, sanitation engineers with sanitation engineers, and so forth.

---

1. You may wish to send for a free copy of the famous appetizer recipe booklet *Appetizers avec Classe.* Available from Bottoms Up Beverage Company, P.O. Box 1412, NY, NY 10022.

DINNER DRIVELRY (OR PRANDIAL PATTER)

- *Do not* avoid controversial subjects. Politics, religion, and sex should be the foundation on which you build a stairway of conversation. Certainly, some people will venture only a few steps at first, others will climb halfway, and some will vault clear to the top. But you will find that those that seemed timid at first will, as the conversation heats up, go bouncing right up those conversational stairs. That's when the fun begins. Once the guests start to get hostile and begin to throw croutons at each other, you will know your party is a success.
- Dinner conversation should be like a good football game—the ball should move up and down the field, not stay at one end. Heated arguments, controversy, name calling, backbiting, ethnic slurs—all help to keep the conversational ball moving. Once that ball stops moving you can fold up the coffee tables.
- A good hostess will not let the dinner conversation wane. If a wane starts to loom, immediately ask everyone to switch seats. This will push a new spirit into the party and generate new and fresh conversational topics.
- "Small talk" must be absolutely forbidden. Nothing is ever accomplished by discussing kids, alimony, former wives, sports, or the weather. Meaty subjects, like Lech Walesa, Prince Andrew, Communism, "60 Minutes" (especially Mike Wallace), and Victoria Principal, are *meaty*.
- If you plan ahead, dinnertime small talk can be nipped in the taste buds before it gets out of hand. A day before the party, draw up a list of Meaty Topics and make a copy of the list for each guest. If small talk should start to rear its ugly pinhead, pass out the Meaty Topics sheets, and then watch things perk up.

CONVERSATION APRÈS DINNER (OR POSTPRANDIAL PATTER)

Furniture placement and conversation go foot-in-sock. For example, the host who entertains in a "conversation pit" has a startling advantage over the poor slob who entertains with metal folding chairs. A conversation pit is a gigantic sofa that consists of many modular units that fit together in thousands of combinations to form yards and yards of upholstery, interrupted only by fall-through cracks. The various units can be arranged for intimate tête-à-têtes, or for an *une*-on-*une* heated debate. Be sure to map out the placement of the modulars the day before the party. (*Note:* It is not necessary to use an "actual size" map of the furniture—a scaled-down version will do.) Do the people-placement on the map, keeping in mind guests with long or short legs, divorced coming as single, married coming as single, former business partners, those with weak kidneys, known-duds, known-comics, and know-it-alls.

While everyone is still at the dinner table, sneak into the living room, or wherever your conversation pit is located (some people have them in the bedroom), and pin place cards to the modular units. (*Note:* Should you be among the unfortunate few saddled with the mundane—a typical three-cushion sofa and a sprinkling of hard and soft chairs, you're on your own—make the best of a bad situation.

Here is an excellent modular sofa plan that was given to us by Charlette Champêtre, a noted conversationalist. Charlette insists that this plan is foolproof no matter what the guest mix is.

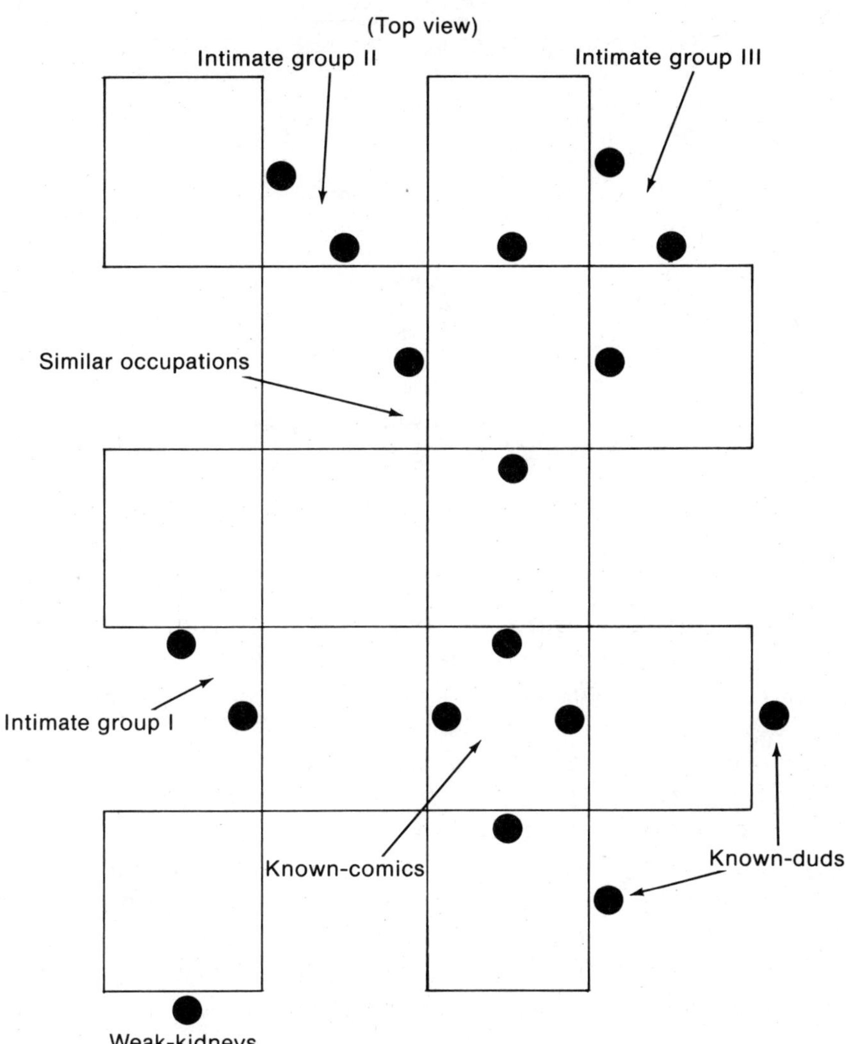
(Top view)
Intimate group II
Intimate group III
Similar occupations
Intimate group I
Known-comics
Known-duds
Weak-kidneys

To some people an egg is an egg. This is an error. Two eggs laid at the same moment, one by a hen that runs loose in the garden, the other by one that feeds in the henyard, can be utterly different in flavor.

Alexandre Dumas *Fils*

17

ALL MYTHED UP

Whenever Real Gourmets congregate, the conversation is heavily laden with food talk. Stories about food bounce around like overcooked abelskivers. There is always scorching controversy about the origins of food and food terms: Which country originated a certain sauce or dish? Which President first brought back from what country this or that food? Which Indian tribe was the first to plant which vegetable? The stories are told, changed, retold, and changed again. Finally, the truth gets so mucked up that no one really knows the truth from the apocrypha.

It is important that the *real truth* be told. Here for the first time are the facts about the origins of certain foods and food terms.

Space does not permit the clearing of the air on everything; for explanations on those left out, drop a postcard to:

Myth Demeanor Press
PO Box 4
Bangor, ME

I urge all Real Gourmets, in the meantime, to continue to seek out the truth in matters of food and drink.

Al Dente—This overused term is actually the name of a dentist in Rhinebeck, New York. Dr. Dente (known to his patients as Dr. Al) has, for many years, encouraged his patients to eat food cooked "to the tooth," meaning slightly past the raw stage. Dr. Dente knew that, when they adopted this method of cooking, his patients returned with more frequency for teeth repair.

Anchovy—The anchovy is a small fish with a curled shape whose native habitat is the olive. The best way to catch an anchovy is to stab it with a toothpick. Anchovies are usually found languishing on top of pizzas and Caesar salads.

Almond—A description used in romantic novels to describe the shape of the eyes of the best-looking woman in the book.

Cabbage—A vegetable of the Ubiquitous family that has been around since the pre-Christian era. Wild claims about its powers as a cure for freckles, hangovers, and infertility are all false. It is well known, however, that pure cabbage juice cures athlete's foot, and that cooked cabbage heightens the sense of smell.

Corn—Without question, the most ancient of vegetables. Ears of corn, dating back to 5000 B.C., have been found in old Mexican caves. Writings on the walls of those caves indicate that the expressions, "corny," "cornball," "cornfed," "corn flakes," and "succotash" date back to that time period.

Cucumber—Many people believe the cuke to be a vegetable, when in fact, it is really a fruit; one that dates back some three thousand years. The name stems out of the northern Indian name *Ucum*, which means *Stupid Banana.*

Eggplant—In ancient times, it was believed that eating

eggplant would make you crazy; there may be some basis of truth here. Melanzana is the Italian word for eggplant, the rough translation of which is "crazy apples." In June, 1958, one Joey Carbone ate six orders of eggplant parmigiana at one sitting and subsequently tried to drive his taxi up the side of the Empire State Building.

Macaroni—(*pastus stringus*)—Let's lay the macaroni myth to rest once and for all: Marco Polo did not bring anything back from Cathay except smallpox. Furthermore, a tree would not have survived that long journey. That's correct, a *tree!* Few people realize that macaroni comes from trees (see photo).

Real Gourmet food doesn't grow on trees, but pasta does. The best macaroni is, of course, hand-picked.

The first macaroni tree was bearing its treasure for the enjoyment of the Italians some thirty years before Mr. Polo went to China. This is a fact that is fully supported by the ancestors of Guilio Spaghetti, who is credited with cultivating the first macaroni tree.

Old books, still in the family archives, show drawings of workers picking the macaroni trees at harvest time, workers laying out the macaroni for drying, and the macaroni during its maturation period.

Many people mistakenly believe that green macaroni is made with spinach, when actually it is really unripe macaroni. It is sometimes picked at the green stage, say when it is being shipped to China; by the time it arrives there, it has ripened to a nice yellow color and is ready for cooking.

Menu—The menu (*escriteau* in old French) is gradually being replaced by "the daily specials" in restaurants. Not too many people order food from the menu anymore. The daily specials are made to sound much more exciting than the menu items, and the prices tacked onto the daily specials are usually four to five dollars higher than anything on the menu. The offering of a menu to diners is now more symbolic than functional.

Oysters (French—*huître;* Italian—*ostrica;* Serbo-Croat—*ostriga*)—Oyster seeds (see photo) are sowed in the bays along the Atlantic Ocean and the Gulf of Mexico. When the young oysters—known as oysterettes—are six to seven weeks old they are harvested and transported to farms in the Rocky Mountains for fattening and plumping. Hence the term *Rocky Mountain oysters.*

Snails (*uglious crawlus*)—Snails are better known as *escargot* in Real Gourmet Restaurants. Many people are of the belief that snails are French in origin. This is sheer folly. The real truth is that snails were a delicacy of the Ancient Romans, and the phrase "an army travels on its

A mature oyster is shown alongside young oysters (oysterettes).

stomach" came forth during the time when Caesar invaded Gaul.[1]

To provide food for the march into France, Caesar's armies were closely followed by millions of snails. The snails—tended to by trained snail herders—were as prized as gold. At the end of the day's march each soldier was issued a ration of six snails for the evening meal.[2] Several of the sharper Centurions were given the task of maintaining an accurate day-by-day count of the

---

1. See photo for authentication of this statement. Also, the Latin phrase "a passo di lumacus" (at a snail's pace) came into being at this time.
2. Many of the more gifted soldiers created some interesting snail dishes; Mock Snails is one example. For recipes, refer to *De Re Culinaria,* a fine example of an early cookbook, written by Coelius Apicus, one of the Apicus brothers. (The Apicuses were noted more for their gluttony than for anything else.)

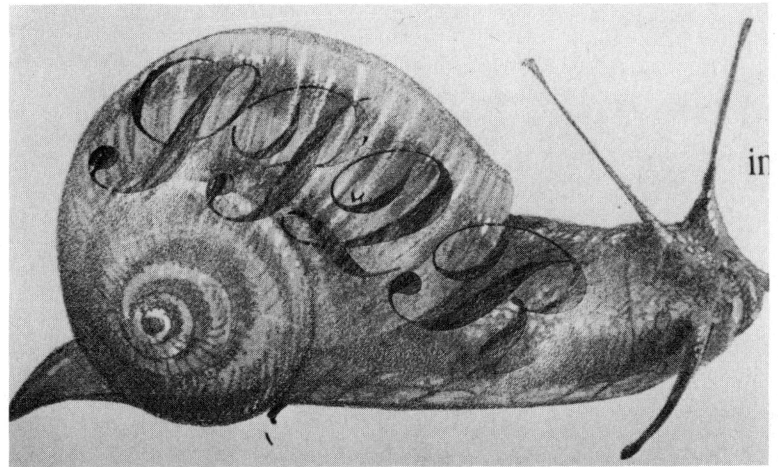

Despite the French name *escargot,* snails actually can be traced back to Ancient Rome.

number of snails consumed, the number remaining, and a projection of the number needed to complete the march.

Tomato (*hivus redus*)—The tomato is actually the fruit of a plant that was considered to be deadly poisonous back in the 15th century. Spaniards, searching for gold in Peru, came across the "golden apple"; hence the Latin name for the tomato—*pomodoro.* The French called the tomato *pommes d'amour,* or "love apples." The discovery of this "apple" caused a real culinary flap all over Europe. Fanciful "apple" dishes began to pop up all over the Continent. In England, Sir Walter Raleigh presented the "apple" to his queen, and her chef created the first "apple tart," not realizing that the "apple" he was using was in fact a tomato.

You are thinking ahead, and you are absolutely right—pizza was first made in England. It wasn't until several years later than an English sailor, stranded in Naples and penniless, started selling pizza (then known

Tomato "pi."

as apple pie). When the error was discovered, the name of the dish was changed to tomato pie.

Truffles (*fungus oakus*)—No one, it seems, has been able to solve the mystery of truffles. What makes them grow under the soil? How do they germinate? What freak of nature causes them to be found only under certain kinds of trees? Why only in France and Italy?

The truth is, they are semi-petrified potatoes. In the 16th and 17th centuries farmers in France and Italy planted their potatoes around and under oak, elm, and willow trees. During the potato harvest potatoes that had a bit of rot were not picked up; they were thrown back and covered with soil. The ensuing years caused them to wrinkle, shrink, and mature into an edible delicacy. The fact that truffles are sniffed out by dogs and pigs—great lovers of potatoes—supports this truth. Truffles are not found in the United States because potatoes are planted in open fields, not under trees.

Walnuts (*noce*)—Walnuts were a food sanctified by the Ancient Romans—food for the gods; "the nuts of Jupiter," they were called. Roman legionnaires introduced them to Great Britain, and they were carried throughout the world on English trading ships. This gave birth to the term "those English nuts," which is still in use today.

As stated before, many foods have been said to contain aphrodisiac powers. To set the record straight, here is the complete list of those that are, and those that are not.

Aphrodisiacs	*Non-aphrodisiacs*
apples	French food
cheese	walnuts
lemons	oysters
chili peppers	vanilla beans
garlic	caraway seeds
kiwi fruit	quiches
marshmallows	egg rolls
peanuts	chicken soup
twinkies	key lime pie
baked clams oreganato	goat cheese
pasta	jalapeño peppers
cheese cake	carrot cake
carrots	German food
Italian food	Russian food
Mexican food	English food
Greek food	

All passions, rationalised and controlled, become an art. Gastronomy, more than any other passion, is sensitive to reasoning and direction.

Monselet
Lettres à Emilie

18

COOKING SCHOOLS

Well over 80 percent of all the Real Gourmets in the United States have attended a cooking school. There is intense enthusiasm, particularly among Real Gourmets, for learning the basic methods and techniques of good cooking. This lust to learn has given birth to cooking schools of every type; and teaching people how to knead, cut, chop, slice, boil, bake, and handle every imaginable kitchen task has become big business.

Students will travel anywhere—abroad, to remote islands, to mountain tops, to emerging nations, and even into emerging neighborhoods—to hone their culinary skills.

Students will pay almost any price to learn how to dazzle their friends, spouses, mothers-in-law, and business associates with their expertise at the piano.[1]

The Official Gourmet Handbook has selected five of the more interesting schools (from the thousands out there) for your consideration. *The Official Gourmet Handbook* does not endorse the schools listed, nor do we feel that they are necessarily the best the world has to offer.[2]

1. Piano is the term used in France for *stove*. An apprentice chef in France has to peel a lot of onions before he gets a chance to "play at the piano."
2. The best cooking school in the world, in our opinion, is the Mellon School of the Culinary Arts. Located in Fargo, North Dakota, the Mellon School teaches every phase of cooking, from *abaisse* (rolled-out pastry), to zwieback (a rusk). Mellon School graduates are working in some of the finest restaurants in the world. And more than 3,000 employees of McDonald's are proud graduates of the Mellon School.

Pope John smiles beatifically over one of the luscious creations he teaches students to prepare at Cucina del Papa.

CUCINA DEL PAPA

His Eminence, Pope John Paul, invites all Americans—regardless of religion or culinary leaning—to the Papal Cooking School. Classes will be conducted right in the Papal Kitchens and taught by Pope John Paul himself.

Surrounded by the great works of Michelangelo, DaVinci, Bernini, et al., students will be inspired to a new level of culinary artistry.

Included in this week-long, hands-on, intensified course in *Ital-o-Poli* cooking are:

- a ride in the papal jeep
- a picnic in the Colosseum
- seminars on the eating habits of the Ancient Romans
- two free bottles of Brioschi
- an assortment of souvenirs

Classes will be conducted in (choose one): (a) Italian, (b) Polish, (c) English, (d) Latin.

The *basso, basso,* all-inclusive price for this exciting week in Rome and environs is only 28 million lira.

For more information, write to:
Msgr. Buono Forchetta
Via Sistine, 12
Rome, Italy

"A heavenly experience. Without a doubt, the best papal cooking school in Italy."

James Beard

Faculty advisors at L'École l'Esprès.

L'ÉCOLE L'EXPRÈS
Correspondence Cooking School
À LA FRANÇAISE
Ashimata Way, 10
Tokyo, Japan

Now you can learn to cook *à la mode Française* without leaving your kitchen. Six of the three-star chefs of France have joined together to form l'École l'Exprès, a premier correspondence cooking school. Have your finished dishes critiqued by these great chefs and find out what you are doing wrong. They will mark your dishes and return them to you with their personal comments.

COMPLETE KIT INCLUDES:

- Express mail pouches
- 24 classic three-star recipes
- Step-by-step instructions
- French-English, English-French dictionary
- Valuable restaurant coupons
- Metric conversion chart
- Bumper sticker
- Simulated chef's hat and matching apron
- Two tickets to Craig Claiborne's 75th birthday bash or the Chicago World's Fair, whichever comes first

YES! ENROLL ME AT ONCE IN L'ÉCOLE L'EXPRÈS. ENCLOSED IS MY CHECK FOR $2,950.10 FOR THE COMPLETE KIT AS DESCRIBED ABOVE.

"Definitely the finest French cooking school in the Orient. My hat is off to l'École l'Exprès."

James Beard

Little-known fact: President Ronald Reagan graduated magna cum laude from the U.S. Army Cooking School.

THE U.S. ARMY COOKING SCHOOL

Now, new government regulations have provided for the opening of regional U.S. Army Cooking Schools.

Now, you too can learn the "secrets" of "chow" as eaten by your father and grandfather.

Intensive hands-on classes right in the mess kitchen let you pitch right in and learn by doing.

Learn the secret ingredients in the renowned "K" rations; how to float eggs on a sea of grease; how to make mystery meat, tube steak; the magic of saltpeter; a fast cure for the dreaded GIs; and more!

The six-week saturation course will enable you to turn out real GI chow for your friends and loved ones.

FOR MORE INFORMATION, WRITE:

QUARTERMASTER GENERAL
FT. BENING, GA

Ask for bulletin No. CS264177-8/42C817-64 as amended.

"Long overdue. This is certainly the wave of the future. My full endorsement."

James Beard

The nose knows—or will know, once you've completed the course at Nose École.

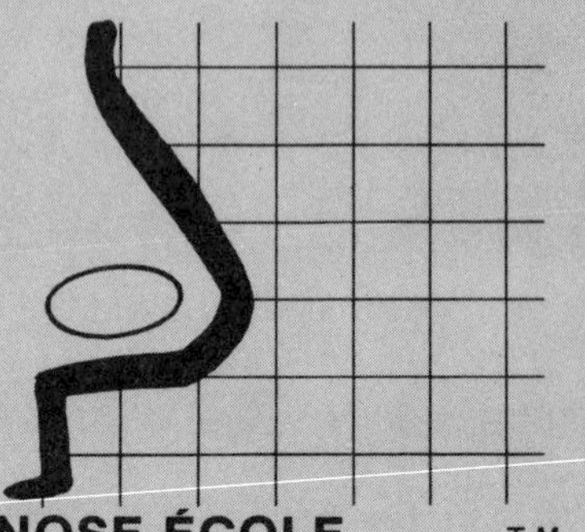

NOSE ÉCOLE T.M.

The world-famous NOSE ÉCOLE is accepting a limited number of applications for training the nose to know fine wines.

Aspiring wine stewards and sommeliers enroll today!

Let us train your nose to sniff out the best in wines. Our eight-week course will qualify you to work in the finest restaurants in this time-honored and high-paying profession.

Learn how to tell REDS FROM WHITES.

Learn how to DECORK AND DECANT.

Learn how to serve WINE IN A BASKET.

Learn how to conduct a harmonious symphony of wine and food.

Learn how to deal with WINE SNOBS.

Learn how to tell a GOOD CELLAR FROM A BAD CELLAR.

FREE PLACEMENT SERVICE
FREE DIPLOMA
FREE LAPEL BADGE
FREE SOMMELIER TASTING CUP
(chain not included)

The complete EIGHT-WEEK course, as described, is only $995.00 (lab materials are extra). For application, write:
NOSE ÉCOLE, 1444 Dexter St., Boston, MA

"This is the finest nose school this side of the Atlantic."

James Beard

STAS STINECKI'S COOKING IN GDANSK

Full-participation cooking classes against a backdrop of muddled politics and political unrest.

Visits to pierogi factories, pig farms, AND MORE!

The lamp-drenched shipyard dinners and a guided tour around a piece of art in the museum are but two of the exciting side trips during this fabulous week in Gdansk.

Learn the intimate secrets of real Polish cooking—wiejska szynka, bigos, chlodnik, Barszcz Wigilijny, and, of course, real kielbasa.

Swim in the Baltic and stare at the Soviets, too!

For more information and free brochure, contact:

ZELDA STINECKI
PO Box 842
Grand Rapids, MI

"Without a doubt the best cooking school in Poland."

James Beard

One of Luigi Benedire's cooking classes receives the customary "official blessing."

LUIGI BENEDIRE'S CUCINA D'ITALIA

T.M.

Luigi Benedire, known throughout the world as the maestro of Italian cooking, is now accepting reservations for his 1988 cooking school program (1984, 1985, 1986, 1987 are sold out). Long hailed as *the* best Italian cooking school, Luigi guides his students through every phase of *cucina d'Italia.* The six-month course starts right here in the United States: Luigi will meet all his students (42 maximum) in Fort Worth, Texas, for a tour of Italian restaurants in that city, to show them what *bad* Italian cooking is all about. ("A frame of reference," says Luigi.) From Ft. Worth, students will jet directly to Milan, where the class will receive the "official blessing." After the blessing students will board Luigi's "kitchen on wheels," a luxurious autobus with a complete kitchen.

La Volante Cucina—"The Flying Kitchen"—will then begin its weave through all of Italy, hitting 63 cities, 28 vineyards, 12 pasta factories, olive oil plants, museums, statues, ruins, restaurants (all classes), bakeries, the Fiat assembly plant, shops, shoe stores, leather factories. In between all these exciting jaunts are the cooking classes, conducted right on the bus—so every moment is fully utilized.

Don't miss out on the *eccitazione*—Sign up today!

All-inclusive price is only $18,000.00. Send for details: Luigi Benedire, PO Box 317, Troy, NY 14177.

"My good friend Luigi has created the finest traveling cooking school in the world. What a genius!"

James Beard

The destiny of nations depends on their manner of eating.

Brillat-Savarin
The Physiology of Taste (1825)

19

COOKBOOKS

New cookbooks roll into the bookstores at the rate of some 300 a year. The number of recipes from all the cookbooks ever printed would fill all the taco shells made in the United States and Mexico since they started making tacos. Cookbooks come in all shapes and sizes—some even in the shape of taco shells. Cookbooks cover every type of cuisine, from Armenian to nouvelle Zen. Cookbooks treat every food ever known, from abalone to zuppa Inglese. There are cookbooks written by chefs, restaurant owners, farmers, politicians, movie stars, rock stars, Yellow Pages salesmen, housewives, aunts, uncles (one of my favorite "uncle books" is *The Pleasures of Provolone* by Zio Granciporo).

As many of you know, I am the cookbook reviewer for the food magazine *The Food Magazine.* During the 20 years that I have been on the job I have reviewed some 8,000 cookbooks. I would like to share with you some past reviews (and one current one) of some of my favorite cookbooks. These, to me, are the best. They exemplify what good cookbook writing is all about; they are the whipped *crème de la crème,* the caviar and champagne, *la meglio di meglio!*

Those of you who are Real Gourmets may already have these cookbooks; those of you who are aspiring gourmets should add these to your cookbook collection.

Nobody Knows the Truffles I've Seen Cookbook by *Paul Becausé*

Right off, I must say that this is a smashing cookbook! Who would have thought that this "diamond of the soil"—*la truffe*—had the makings of a full-blown cookbook? Plaudits must go to M. Becausé for even attempting to address this difficult—but, oh, so tasty—subject.

M. Becausé is the owner of the world-famous three-star restaurant La Maison de la Mère et Père, near Verbe Irrégulier, in the South of France (Highway N2). He also holds the four-flags, six-toques, four-geese, seven-swans, and eight maids-a-milking restaurant awards.

"We use *la truffe* in almost every dish we cook at LMMP," he told me. And use *la truffe* he does, in this shining work. M. Becausé discusses all types of truffles—black, white, and the new pink hybrid. (I personally feel that he made an unjustified attack on Italian truffles, and I have written a letter to him on the subject.)

In his book M. Becausé decries the use of canned truffles. "It's like substituting catfish for Dover Sole," he admonishes. Here is one of the toothsomely palatable recipes from this *première classe* cookbook.

Truffe au Champagne Becausé

4 pounds of fresh truffles, peeled*
1 cup mirepoix of vegetables, cooked until soft
6 cups dry champagne
6 tablespoons thick brown veal stock

Put the well-cleaned truffles into a deep saucepan with the mirepoix. Add the champagne. Cook, covered, over medium heat for 15 minutes. Remove the truffles to a deep dish. Boil the pan juices down to nothing (almost); add to the pan juices the veal stock. Mix well. Sprinkle the truffles with this mixture. Cover the dish and cook over low heat (not boiling) for 7 minutes. Serve at once.

*Reviewer's note: it is customary to use *unpeeled* truffles for this dish. Let your palate guide you accordingly.

The Dr. Guilio Pearlman with the University of Krakow–Extension Diet Cookbook

Advance note: The September 1984 issue of *The Food Magazine* will do an in-depth focus report on this revolutionary new diet cookbook. Because my personal test results were so startling, I am giving you this prereview.

Ho-hum! Another diet book. That's what I thought when I received galley proofs from the publisher just the other day. My ho-hum did a sharp U-turn into *mmmmmms* shortly into the first chapter. This is it! I said to myself. Finally, someone has come up with a diet book that makes sense. No calorie counting, no exercises, no bean sprouts, no vitamin supplements, no yogurt. Dr. Guilio Pearlman, you are truly a savior.

To think that the real secret to losing weight—tons of it—boils down, quite simply, to Polish sausage! It seems that there is something in Polish sausage that melts fat off the human body. Dr. Pearlman, and nutritionists at U of K, came upon this phenomenon by pure accident. After three years of disciplined testing, using real people from the Tatra Mountains in the south of Poland, they released their results in this bombshell-of-a-diet cookbook.

Simply stated, the more Polish sausage one eats, the more weight one loses. A simple, straightforward diet—and it works!

I started the PUKE (Pearlman University Krakow Extension) Diet on a Monday morning; Thursday at noon (the same week), I was 14 pounds lighter. Had I continued the diet, I might have slipped through a crack in my kitchen floor.

The book is filled with delicious, taste-bud-tingling recipes, all using Polish sausage (also known as kielbasa). The book is smartly sectioned by time of day so the reader can plan breakfast, lunch, and dinner meals without falling into intolerable boredom.

A word of caution is given in the book: "Two weeks on and two weeks off," or the author and the U of K cannot be responsible for acute thinness.

Readers would do well to take advantage of the special "cents off" coupons for Polish sausage in the back of the book.

Nouvelle Mondo Cookbook by *Agnes Dittle*

Until the time this cookbook came out, the name Agnes Dittle was little known; now it's a household word. The success of this book has moved Agnes Dittle center-stage and then some. She has appeared on the "Good Morning America" and "Today" shows. She has guest-hosted "The Tonight Show." She has her own cooking show on public television. "I was just a frumpy housewife until my book came out," she told me.

It's been quite a year for Agnes, but then, Agnes wrote quite a cookbook. (It's being considered by NBC for a miniseries.) The epiclike sweep of this book (it's 1,874 pages long, has more than 6,000 recipes, 1,500 photographs, and weighs just under 36 pounds) is breathtaking and mouth-watering. Ms. Dittle covers every conceivable food from every country, nation, continent, hemisphere, and principality. Every part of the world is given equal treatment, including all the emerging nations.

Little-known (but great) recipes abound in this "New World" cookbook. I wish there was space to cover each and every recipe, but there isn't. But here's a good cross-section: from Africa—Gari Foto; from Finland—Keitetyt Ravut; from Russia—Medivnyk; from the Arab States—Samakah Harrah; from the Low Countries—Moules "Le Zoute"; from Bulgaria—Banista; from France—Casse-Museau; from Italy—Nido di Uccello Zuppa; from the United States—regional recipes from every state in the Union. (The Los Angeles recipe is Sprouts à la Bert Convy.) Ms. Dittle took almost a full year to assemble and test each and every recipe. "It was a labor of love," she said. Throw out all your cookbooks; this is the only one you'll need.

The Complete Fusilli Cookbook by *Matreselva* "Honeysuckle" *Rosa*

Fusilli, the most ubiquitous pasta, is finally trapped and tamed by Signora Rosa in this marvelous cookbook. Inspired by her husband's love for fusilli—Signor Rosa eats it six times a week—she created hundreds of dishes using this delectable spiral-shaped pasta.

Signora Rosa, prompted by friends and relatives to open her fusilli treasure trove to the world, brought forth this jewel of a book that exposes facets of fusilli that have never been considered heretofore.

Here is just a sampling of some fabulous fusilli dishes that are in this formidable cookbook: Fusilli Benito, Fusilli con Fusilli, Stuffed Fusilli, Breaded Fusilli, Braided Fusilli, Next-Day Fusilli, Fusilli Grasso Stupido (Fat-Head Fusilli, named in honor of her husband), and my favorite, Cold Fusilli Stuffed with Garlic.

It is safe to say that anybody who loves pasta will love this book.

Signora Rosa, boosted by the enormous success of her fusilli book, is now working on Volume I of her new pasta series—*Spaghetti, Another Turn, Another Time.*

One Thousand and Two of the World's Most Difficult Recipes—Made Easy—Cookbook by *Harvey Easemark*

Mr. Easemark spent some 30-odd years in kitchens around the world—from the prisons of France to the galley of H.M.S. *Ralph.* Faced with complex and impossible situations through these cooking years, Mr. Easemark became a master at coping with the ridiculous and an expert in contrivance. Filled with this knowledge (and just hanging around the house after his retirement), Mr. Easemark's wife, Toasty, urged him to write this all-consuming cookbook.

And write he did, by God! Mr. Easemark shows with ease how to make mincemeat out of some of the most complex dishes ever to be set before king or commoner.

For example, his detailed, yet simple and concise, approach to "A Peacock Dinner for 27" goes so far as to explain where to find peacocks and how to pluck them. His simplified handling of a "Double Souffle" (Soufflé en Soufflé), is a masterful unwinding of a complex dessert. Also, the easy-to-follow instructions on how to track and cook a yak is refined simplicity. And, to say the least, the Mock Béchamel Sauce is truly the work of a genius. Mr. Easemark is a cook who knows his "piano" from his violin.

The Complete Book of Beans by *Piero Fagiolino*

Piero Fagiolino is an author who uses his beans—30 different varieties at that—in this exciting *Book of Beans.* Blue pea, mung, split mung, skinless mung, and urd are just a few. Black, Borlotto & White, by coincidence, are Signor Fagiolino's attorneys, which has nothing to do with the book, but it's interesting to note that those are the names of beans.

Signor Fagiolino's book is heaped with explosive information about beans: growing, picking, storage, soaking, cooking, preserving, necklace making, shelling, nutrition, etc. One of the most interesting chapters is the one that explains the effect that beans had on the outcome of World War II.

Truly, this book is a must for the consummate bean eater; easy-to-follow recipes and a bean indentification chart add to the strength of the presentation. This book blows away the clouds of mystery that have surrounded the "common bean," and truly makes it a snap for the beginning bean cook to plunge in and start cooking.

Three cheers and a hearty whistle blast for this long-overdue book.

The discovery of a new dish does more for the happiness of mankind than the discovery of a star.

Brillat-Savarin
The Physiology of Taste (1825)

20

RECIPES

Real Gourmets love to exchange recipes to reveal to others their expertise in the culinary arts.

Food sections of newspapers around the country are a hotbed of recipe swapping.

Food magazines openly solicit, and often pay big money for, recipes from their readers.

Many of these recipes are interesting, exciting, new, and without question, the real food that is being cooked and served throughout the United States. I have selected a sampling of the more imaginative ones that I have collected over the years from newspapers and food magazines.

If you have an exciting recipe based on "good ol' All-American cooking," send it along. If it passes our blue-ribbon panel of taste-testers, I will include your recipe in my new book—*Red, White, and Chew.*

AN OSCAR WINNER

When I prepare hamburgers, everyone loves them, including our dog Oscar. Let me share this treasured recipe with you.

Hamburger Oscar

Make the hamburger patties: Open one package (16 ounces) of ground beef. Shape the meat into rounds of 4 ounces each. Place on a baking sheet. Broil for 2–3 minutes on each side. Serve on toasted sesame seed buns. *Serves 4.*

Stan Fryburger
Altoona, PA

ZIP, ZAP, AND SERVE

I was the proud recipient of the first microwave oven on our block (from my husband). This dish is a favorite at my monthly "Microwave Magic" parties.

Micro-Cheese Melts Lucy

Open a package of sliced white bread; cut off the crust. Pipe a good brand of pimiento cheese-in-a-tube around the edge of each slice. Put a slice of tomato in the center of each bread slice. Pipe more cheese, in the shape of a fleur de lis, on each tomato. Place the bread slices in a microwave oven and zap them for 40–50 seconds or until the fleur de lis loses its identity. Serve at once. *Serves one block.*

Lucy Meltos
Kewaunee, WI

THE HEIGHT OF SUCCESS

I am enclosing a recipe for a fortune cookie cake that was handed down from a construction worker on the 80th floor of the World Trade Center when it was being built. It is a real favorite at our *maison.*

A Fortunate Cookie Cake

Crush 36 fortune cookies (reserve the fortunes) by pounding them with the flat side of a cleaver. Place the crushed cookies in a mixing bowl. Stir in 1 cup of melted margarine and mix thoroughly. Mold the cookie mixture into an 8¼-inch greased springform pan. Make 1 package chocolate pudding mix according to directions, but leave out step 3. Pour the pudding mixture into the springform pan and chill for 2 hours. Roll the paper fortunes into tubes to resemble candles. Insert the fortunes vertically into the pudding. At serving time, light the fortunes and rush to the table. *Serves 8.*

Linda Too-Fro
NY, NY

SOUTH OF THE BORDER

I have been enjoying your magazine since shortly after the Civil War. And even though we lost, I still respect your integrity. Let me share this "field dish" that still gets raves on either side.

Mason-Dixon Mix, Bobby Jo

Dig a pit exactly 2 feet deep and 1½ feet in diameter in red clay soil. Line the pit with aged oak boards. Over a wood fire, in a big pot, bring 22 pounds of choice hominy to a full boil. Pour the hominy into the pit. Stir well. Sprinkle ½ cup grated Parmesan cheese on top. Cover with canvas. Let sit for 3 days. Cut into bite-sized wedges. Garnish. *Serves many.*

Bobby Jo Dixon
Mason, GA

HUE-RAY FOR PARSLEY

We enjoyed a parsley salad at the house of a friend. (It was really terrible, but we told her we enjoyed it.) But being a creative cook (my husband's words), I made a few changes and came up with a lip-smacking winner.

Parsley Tree à la House

Cut the base off a large melon. Punch holes all around the melon exactly $\frac{1}{16}$ inch apart, in rows ¼ inch apart, in perfect circles. Dye 3 bunches of washed parsley in food coloring: red, yellow, brown, and blue. Insert the stems of the parsley into the holes, mixing the colors as you go. Freeze for 2 hours. Sprinkle with powdered sugar. *Serves 14.*

Buffy House
Wheaton, IL

FOUR-ALARM FLAMBÉ

My husband loves to flambé (he took lessons at Arthur Murray's), and this dish is a step and away his best ever and we are grateful contributors.

Ole Flambé Mole

Peel 7 bananas. Marinate them for 3 days in 2 copitas of a great Oloroso sherry. At serving time, tableside, stand the bananas on end in a chafing dish. Place a slice of orange on the tip of each banana; top the orange slice with a Maraschino cherry. Pour ½ bottle of dark imported rum over the bananas. Step back 3 paces, light a match, and throw it into the chafing dish. As the dish is flaming, all the guests do intricate dance steps around the chafing dish while chanting "Ole Mole!" *Serves 2–10.*

Ole Mole
El Paso, TX

FOUR-WHEEL CHILI

Our chili parties are famous. The enclosed letters from our thousands of friends bear that out. We love your magazine and want to share our recipe with fellow readers and lovers of *hot* cuisine.

Pickup Chili Cartwright

Line the back of a pickup truck with a heavy plastic drop cloth. Pour in 24 no. 20 cans of tomatoes, 18 pounds of prime beef (diced), 4 cups of assorted herbs and spices. Drive the truck over rough terrain for 12 miles. Move a flame thrower slowly around the sides of the truck until the chili is bubbly and the meat cooked. Just before serving, fold in ½ bushel of chopped green peppers and onion. *Serves a bunch.*

"Tubs" Cartwright
El Paso, TX

HEIRLOOM SAUSAGE

My great aunt, Sally, kept this recipe a closely guarded secret until her death; it was finally revealed at the reading of her will. I would now like to share it with the world.

Silly Sausage Sally

Prepare 2 pounds of hog casings or make your own. Chop and mince ½ cup each of the following: Beri-Beri nuts, miniature marshmallows, ginger snaps, old Peking duck, and Agaricus Campestris. Fold the first ingredient into the second, the second into the third, and so forth. Using a wooden dowel, stuff the mixture into the casings until you run out of casings or filling. Tie the sausage into links using various colors of string. Hang the sausage to dry for 2 weeks in a white pine barn (if white pine is not available, substitute alder). Broil or sauté when ready. *Serves ?*

Bertha Farcito
Morris, NJ

A little wine is a dangerous thing; but 'tis better to have tried the wine than never to have drunk at all.

Anonymous

21

WINE BIBBER'S BASICS AND WINE BIBBER'S BABEL

Real Gourmets must have a wine cellar.

•

Real Gourmets must know how to stock and store a wine cellar properly.

•

Real Gourmets must know how to open a wine bottle.

•

Real Gourmets must know about the serving of wine.

•

Let's take these four "wine in action" precepts and discuss them one by one.

WINE CELLAR

By definition a wine cellar is a cellar where wine is stored; a stock of wine. Be assured, two or three bottles of wine do not a wine cellar make; not does a half-gallon of jug wine in the refrigerator.

You must take the time and spend the money to stock and maintain a decent cellar. Your status as a Real Gourmet will be enhanced brilliantly when you say to your dinner guests, "Excuse me, I must go to my wine cellar and select an appropriate wine for dinner."

The Official Gourmet Handbook asked noted wine expert a Confrerie du Tastevin and a member of the Chaine du Gang, Hugh "Corky" Robent, to put together a model wine cellar. Here are his recommendations:

---

6 cases Red Burgundy
6 cases White Burgundy
6 cases Red Bordeaux
3 cases White Bordeaux
1 case Sauterne
2 cases Champagne
2 cases California white
2 cases California red

That adds up to 28 cases. Total investment will run about $6,000, give or take a dollar or two—not too much to ask for this kind of daily pleasure. However, this might be a bit more cork than you wish to pop for, so we asked a noted wine monger for an alternate cellar selection. Here it is:

---

2 cases Hudson Valley Red
2 cases Hudson Valley White
3 cases Italian Red
1 case Italian White
1 case Greek (Roditis is good)
2 bottles Hungarian (Monimpex)
2 bottles German (some type of Rhine)
2 bottles Australian (Yalumba)
4 bottles South African (Klein Karoo)

That adds up to about 10 cases. Total investment will run about $300. The amount of daily pleasure from this selection is not quite as high as from the first, but at least you can say that you have a wine cellar.

STORAGE

Wines should be stored in compartmented shelves, in a cool corner of your cellar (basement), kitchen, living room, or den. You must maintain a constant temperature of 55° F. to keep the wines from being impaired or damaged.

How much space will you need for storage? A formula for this: Add up the total number of bottles. Figure three dozen bottles in a space three feet by three feet. Subtract from that figure your normal consumption for a 30-day period. Then simply add to that figure the number of feet from the wine cellar to your dining room. Keep in mind, however, that the wine must be stored on its side (otherwise your computations may be totally wrong).

OPENING THE BOTTLE

Wine bottles are, as a rule, opened with a device called a *corkscrew.* There are several types of screws on the market: winged, waiter's, machine, ball, and set. Most people prefer the winged for home use.[1]

SERVING WINE

Wine service and handling carry a few easy-to-follow rules:

- Whites and pinks are served chilled.

1. An excellent book—*Pop Goes the Cork*—shows in pictures (more than 120 of them) an easy, step-by-step method of opening a wine bottle. This book is a wise investment for the wine connoisseur.

- Reds should be decorked—decanted too, if you wish—at least two hours before serving to "loosen them up."
- Reds should be served at a temperature of 65° F. (19° C.).
- Reds are never served before whites (this was the problem that led to the Indian uprisings).
- Never serve a red Burgundy before a red Bordeaux, nor a Hudson Valley red before an Italian red.
- Always move from lesser wines to great wines.
- If you overchill a bad white wine, it will taste better (a good rule to follow for all German whites).
- Vinegar and jelly are unfriendly to any wine.
- People who serve ice cubes with wine should be put in a home.
- Wine baskets (for serving red wine) went out with spats.
- Never fill a wine glass to the brim; the reasons are too numerous to mention.
- Wine glass criteria: a wine glass should be tulip shaped, clear, thin, without markings (thought your family crest on your lead-crystal glasses was cute, didn't you?), the bowl the size of a large orange. One glass with those features can serve for all wines, regardless of color or type.

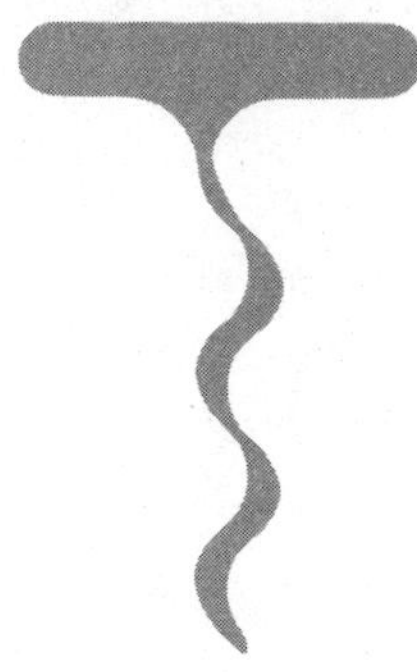

WINE BIBBER'S BABEL— LETTERS FROM READERS

"Wine Bibber's Babel" welcomes comments and questions. For personal reply, send a self-addressed stamped envelope and a $5 bill to : Wine Bibber's Babel, 13 Via Vino, Sonoma, CA. The material and the money become our property and can be used for our personal gain.

My next-door neighbor is into making his own wine. It's the worst wine I have ever tasted. It is not winsome or lively; nor is it playful or seductive. And, worst of all, it has no earthy complexity. In the face of all this, he insists on serving it every time we have dinner at his house. How can I politely tell him that his wine tastes like aged swamp water?
Tony Diaz-Black
Bar Harbor, ME

Home wine making has never produced a wine with the characteristic that you describe—nor will it ever. Making wine at home is playtime for adults who never had a chemistry set when they were kids. The old Italians knew how to make a good "Dago red" by taste and instinct. Reading a book on home wine making doesn't cut it.

Why don't you tell him that his wine tastes like aged swamp water? You probably won't be invited to dinner again, but then his cooking is probably as bad as his wine.

What is Sangria?
Julio Rosenberg
New York, NY

Sangria is a wine drink of Spanish origin. The name stems

from the Spanish word sangre, *which means* blood. *Sangria is made with red wine, citrus fruit, sugar, and brandy. Choice vintages are all even-numbered years from 1982 on. Foods compatible with Sangria are: twinkies, marshmallows, foil-wrapped candy, and all fruits that begin with a* W.

I have a bottle of Chianti wine that has been in my family for several generations. The label reads: CARRETTO a MANO VINO. IMBOTTIGLIATO NELLA CASA DEL VECCHIO BARCOLLANTE. Can you tell me if this is a rare old wine, and, if so, what it is worth?
Fangoso Acqua
San Francisco, CA

Hold on tight to that bottle! You have a rare bottle of Italian wine. It is worth about $20,000. The translation of your label is: "Pushcart wine. Bottled in the house of a shaky old man." Pushcart wine was made in very limited quantities by early Italian immigrants that knew how to make classic red wine. The selling of "pushcart" wine stopped shortly after the famous "pushcart wars" of 1897, which decimated the "fleet."

I am interested in purchasing a vineyard in northern California. It should have a minimum of 10,000 acres with mature vines, a winery, landing strip, and other basic amenities. Price is no object. Can you help?
Prince Fiz Ben-Big
Saudi Arabia

Well, that's a pretty tall order, Prince. You might start by contacting E&J Gallo, Coca-Cola, Almaden, Nestle Co., Christian Brothers, and others of that ilk. Wineries of the size you are looking for are not usually listed with the local Century 21 real estate person. You may have to do a bit of digging on your own. We'll pass on anything we hear, though.

My wife and I are always looking for new and interesting wines. Can you recommend three or four emerging wineries of note in the United States?
Mike and Irene Blueberry
The Hamptons

Yes, we can! It seems that there is a varietal of these vineyards cropping up every seven years or so. Here are some that may be of interest: Cult Cellars, near Mendocino in northern California, known for fine ceremonial wines. Frog's Leap Winery, Hudson River Valley area (first-rate apple and cherry wines just now coming to the market). Villa Vino, in the Catskill Mountains, is producing some excellent cabarets. (sic) Murphy's Vineyards, Hyannisport, MA. This small winery makes a nice Irish Rose that goes great with salt water taffy.

My fiancé and I were dining out, and I asked her to select the wine. She made an excellent choice and gave the order to the captain-cum-wine-steward. The captain then presented the label to me for inspection and poured some wine into my glass for approval. How should I have handled this gaffe?
Mitch Bradley III
Boston, MA

Restaurants in general, and captains in particular, have yet to cross the bridge of equal rights when it comes to the women's role in a restaurant situation. They assume that the man must order the wine, that a woman doesn't have any grape lore whatsoever. There were two possible ways to have handled the situation: forcefully berating the captain for a breach of wine protocol ("the person ordering the wine approves the wine"); or telling the captain that you would like to whisper something to him; when his ear was near your mouth, you should have given it a good bite.

● ● ●

APPENDIX A:

TALK OF THE TRADE

Now that you have studied *The Official Gourmet Handbook,* you may be close to achieving Real Gourmet status. To reach the level of Real Gourmet, and to make sure that title and distinction are conferred on you by your friends (or to dub *yourself* Real Gourmet) won't be easy—reading this book is just a start.

There will be endless days and nights of reading food magazines, wine magazines, and food and wine magazines. There will be the seemingly endless clipping of recipes from newspapers; the swapping of I-can't-wait-to-try-this-recipe with friends and neighbors; the forsaking of hours with the television soaps for hours with the kitchen stove; the weekly reading, column by column, of the food section in the newspaper; the challenge to your mate, "What do you want, Real Gourmet food or sex? You can't have both." Yes, becoming a Real Gourmet isn't easy, but you stay with it. You must stay with it; otherwise you will never pass Real Gourmet; and, if you don't pass Real Gourmet, you can't move on to Epicure; and without Epicure, Gastronome will be nothing more than an elusive dream.

You know what it's going to

take: You must read about recipes, not romance. You must make dish after dish—not the mundane, but the spectacular. You must have a food processor, not a blender. You must go to cooking schools, domestic and international. You must have a kitchen full of the best in pots and pans. You must have several drawers filled with kitchen gadgets that do everything from turning radishes into roses to turning a stick of butter into Mr. Rushmore. You must eat in gourmet restaurants as often as possible. And, unless you have eaten in at least one three-star restaurant in Europe, you cannot even begin the arduous trek toward the pinnacle on which Real Gourmets sit and sing.

Those of you who have the burning desire to reach that lofty perch must study, study, and study some more. You must read, read, read, and read again. You must reach out for the knowledge that will elevate you to Real Gourmet status. Whether or not you can reach Epicure or Gastronome status depends solely on the time and money you are willing to expend.

To help you in your quest to reach Real Gourmet status, *The Official Gourmet Handbook*, in conjunction with Citrus Belt State College in Daytona Beach, Florida, has compiled a list of reading material, cooking shows, and gourmet restaurants with which the gourmet aspirant must be familiar.*

READING MATERIAL

Magazines

Gourmet
Bon Appétit
Cuisine
Food & Wine
Fast Food Digest
The Food Magazine
The Pleasures of Cooking
The Cook's Magazine
Travel & Leisure
Wines & Spirits
The Wino's Digest
Range Round Up
Attenzione
Popular Food
Cook's Illustrated
Recipes & Rapport
Cook's Digest
People and Food
Women's Wear Daily

Newspapers

All the newspapers from major cities around the country

*Readers might wish to contact Citrus Belt State College about their classes in Gourmet. The college has classes that lead to a degree in Real Gourmet and postgraduate study for degrees in Epicure and Gastronome. Dial 1-800-G-O-U-R-M-E-T for further information.

should be read. Pay particular attention to the weekly "Food Section."

Cookbooks

See Chapter 19 in this book.

TELEVISION COOKING SHOWS

"The Frigid Gourmet"
"Beat the Pot"
"Family Fuel"
"The Fresh Chef"
"The Pot Watcher" (cable)
"Hu's at the Stove"
"The Farcito Tacchino Show"
"La Vieux Piano"

GOURMET RESTAURANTS

Refer to Chapter 12 in this book, plus the restaurants listed below.

France

Les Frères Douzegros
Le Moulin à Vent
L'Auberge du Lily
Paul Becausé
Beaucoup d'Argent
Donnez-Moi de l'Argent
Chez la Mère Rouge
Fredy le Cervelle
Café la Composition

Italy

Ristorante Pietro & Paolo
Ristorante Giuseppe
Ristorante Giovanni
Mangiare Bene
Ristorante Giorgio
Ristorante Carlo
Ristorante Stappare

APPENDIX B:

GALLERY OF FINE GIFTS AND GOURMET PRODUCTS

Form, function, and fashion are the ingredients in the marinade of style that makes this handbook the most respected resource for finding fine gifts and gourmet products. It features the newest and most innovative products on the market today—products that aspiring gourmets must seriously consider if they plan to work their way out of the morass onto the high and dry ground on which the Real Gourmets sit and bask.

The products on the pages that follow are just a small sampling of what we have to offer. For example, our Lobster Farm Kit for raising live lobsters at home comes complete with lobster tank, lobster seedlets, lobster food, and recipe booklet. Just think, in a few short weeks you can be eating fresh lobsters, right from your own lobster farm. Or order our 12-piece kit for cleaning ox duodenum or our private collection of half-and-half wines (half red and half white, all in one bottle). All this and much more is fully illustrated in our 278-page catalog. Send for your copy today to:

Gallery of Fine Gifts and Gourmet Products
11 Ol' Lyme Way
Greenwich, CT

Your Cook's Dinnerware Collection can be ordered with the face of James Beard or other famous food people.

THE COOK'S DINNERWARE COLLECTION

Start your collection of COOK'S DINNERWARE today! Presenting your Real Gourmet meals on COOK'S DINNERWARE is a fitting finale to the hard work that went into the preparation of the gourmet meal that your guests will enjoy.

Imagine the exclamations of delight from your guests when they eat their way through a saddle of mutton to reveal a picture of their favorite food person.

Made of high-fired porcelain, COOK'S DINNER-

WARE is delicate but not too dainty and dishwasher safe.

Service for one includes dinner, salad, and bread-and-butter plate, plus cup and saucer. (Your guests will smile knowingly when they see Julia Child smiling at them from the bottom of the coffee cup.) Choose from the following cooks: James Beard (pictured), Julia Child, Jacques Pepin, Craig Claiborne and Pierre Franey (two pictures for the price of one), Paul Bocuse, Fredy Giradet, Ma Tooker, Giuliano Bugialli, Alain Chapel, Roger Verge, the frugal gourmet (Jeff Smith).

Please indicate on your order if you wish to have just one cook on pieces selected, or if you would like us to mix and match. Service for four—$49.99. Accessory pieces: Soup bowl—$12.00, Demitasse set—$9.00, Soup Tureen—$45.00, Large Platter—$95.00 (Large Platter has pictures of all the cooks named, across the center). Order from: The Cuisine Collection, PO Box 271, Mouton-on-the-Hudson, NY 12256. Or dial: D-I-N-N-E-R-W-A-R-E.

WINE-IN-A-BOX

The newest and smartest way to buy wine. WINE-IN-A-BOX is just the thing for picnics, patio parties, mobile homes, and those special moments when wine means so much.

Great for sporting events like polo, cricket, tennis, and bowling as the flat box makes pocket storage a snap, with no fear of bulging pockets; no more worries about bottle breakage either.

Each box comes with a full-length straw; just pop in through the top of the box and sip away. Boxes are

The latest in convenience foods for takeout occasions: wine in a box.

ice chest and refrigerator proof to facilitate chilling.

Each individual box contains a full 750 mls; they are packed 48 to a master case—that's 36,000 mils of pure enjoyment.

Select your favorite wines from the attached order list and price sheet. ORDER NOW—you may be only a sip away from being a Real Gourmet. Note: we are temporarily out of 1970 and 1976 red Bordeaux and 1975 and 1981 Sauternes.

FINGER FORKS

The greatest invention since plastic wrap is now

Throw away your finger bowls and buy a set of these invaluable finger forks.

available to the general public. Up to now, FINGER FORKS were the exclusive property of royalty and were illegal for public use. Recent court decrees have struck down the royal monopoly on this product—so now, you too, can eat like the royals.

Marvelously efficient, FINGER FORKS are just the thing for eating asparagus, carrot sticks, snails, olives, ribs, celery—without messing up the fingers. Practically eliminates the boresome finger bowl, wet-naps, and excessive napkin usage—and will surely send chopsticks the way of the dinosaur.

Simply slip the FINGER FORKS onto your thumb and forefinger and eat with gusto—with no fear of sticky fingers. Babies and young children can master the use of FINGER FORKS in a matter of minutes. Just think, no more messy fingerprints all over the house. Socially acceptable at all levels (they were certainly good enough for the royals).

ORDER TODAY! FINGER FORKS come in small, medium, and large to fit any thumb or finger. Also, you can choose silver, gold, or stainless steel.

Only $6.00 the set (gold and silver slightly higher). Save 20 percent on 12 or more sets. Specify whether you are right-handed or left-handed. Order from:

DIGIMATIC LTD.
14 Cornwall St.
London England NW54ST

WINE VINTAGE VERIFIER

"Simple, Accurate, Foolproof." That's what noted wine expert and oenologist, Bruce Boredough, said

1981
1980
1979
1978
1977
1976
1975
1974
1973
1972
1971
1970
1969
1968
1967
1966
1965
1964
1963
1962
1961
1960
1959
1958
1957
1956
1955

about the WINE VINTAGE VERIFIER.

How many times have you been "soaked" for a bottle of wine that had a top-rated vintage year listed on the label when, in fact, the wine in the bottle was actually a lesser-rated vintage year? Here's how to put an end to that kind of chicanery! Take along several strips of the WINE VINTAGE VERIFIER when you go to a restaurant. When the bottle is opened by the wine steward, simply dip the WINE VINTAGE VERIFIER strip into the bottle. The *actual* year of the wine will be verified because one of the year blocks on the strip will turn orange. That's the year of the wine in the bottle—not what it says on the label on the bottle! The WINE VINTAGE VERIFIER is the only way to avoid wine ripoff and to keep wine bottlers on their toes.

ORDER TODAY: 12 strips to a package—only $29.95 postpaid. Send order to: Wine Vintage Verifier, 12 School St., Kankakee, IL. (Vintage verifiers for years prior to 1955 available on request.)

PROCESSOR GIGANTICA

How many times have you said to yourself "I wish I had a food processor with more capacity"? Wish no more! The PROCESSOR GIGANTICA was designed with the Real Gourmet in mind. Big loads of food processing are a snap with the PROCESSOR GIGANTICA. Process 20 pounds of potatoes, 40 pounds of beans, 15 pounds of pie crust. Slice tomatoes, carrots, and zucchini by the bushel. There's no big job that this "queen of machines" can't accomplish. Had a problem making big batches of pasta dough? The PROCESSOR GIGANTICA can make mounds of macaroni (with optional attachment) in a matter of minutes. BUT WAIT! Don't order yet! The PROCESSOR GIGANTICA comes with a box of 100 40-quart vinyl food bags for easy processing and freezing of all your food. And listen to this—22 quarts of delicious homemade ice cream in just 18 minutes with the optional ice cream attachment. Now what do you

Now you can entertain the entire town without emptying and refilling your food processor. The Processor Gigantica also comes with optional Macaroni and Super-Sucker attachments to make those big cooking jobs a breeze.

think? BUT WAIT! Don't order yet! You not only get the PROCESSOR GIGANTICA, the free food bags, and a 60-day warranty, we'll throw in the fabulous *PROCESSOR GIGANTICA COOKBOOK*—378 pages of culinary heat that will make your tastebuds do a tango all over your tongue. Now how much would you expect to pay? BUT WAIT! If you order today, you'll get the machine, the food bags, the 60-day warranty, and the cookbook, plus, we'll throw in—absolutely free—the sensational SUPER-SUCKER ATTACHMENT, which lets you suck food right out of a bushel basket into the machine without lifting a finger. Now how much would you expect to pay for all of this? $1,500.00, $1,200.00, $1,000.00? How about $850.00? Well, enough suspense—pay only $750.00 and the entire deal is yours. Hard to believe, but true. ORDER NOW by calling 1-800-M-A-C-H-I-N-E. Operators are standing by. (This is a free call.)

THE FABULOUS BUBBLE-PACK-BOIL MEALS

Tired of frozen dinners that run together on the tray, and before you know it the dessert becomes a part of the entrée? Tired of frozen dinners that take forever to cook in the oven? Tire no more! From the commissary of Cuisine Vitesse comes the BUBBLE-PACK-BOIL. Each bubble-pack holds a complete gourmet feast—appetizer, entrée, vegetable, salad, and dessert—each in its own bubble-pack compartment. Just drop the bubble-pack into cold water, bring to a boil, remove from the water, open the bubble-pack with the patented zip-strip, and enjoy.

Look for your favorite meal in the dairy section of your favorite food store: Mexican, Italian, French, and Chinese are all there, plus clam bake bubble-packs, vegetarian bubble-packs, and diet bubble-packs.

Take advantage, too, of our BUBBLE-PACK-MEAL-OF-THE-MONTH-CLUB. Each month, we will send you a surprise gourmet meal, made in our kitchens by a Real Gourmet chef. Or, give as a gift to a Real Gourmet friend or business client. To whet your appetite, here is the MEAL-OF-THE-MONTH that we will be mailing in September.

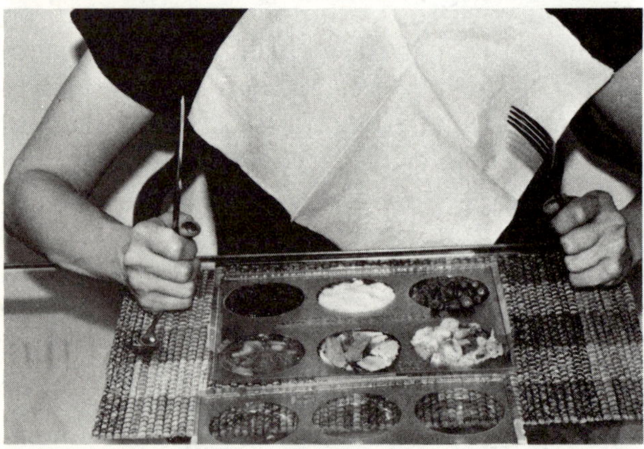

With these ingenious Bubble-Pack-Boil Meals, Real Gourmets can prepare *haute cuisine* faster than they can say "zip-strip."

La Goutte d'Or au Fumet de Cailles
*
La Mousseline de Coquilles St. Jacques—42nd Street
*
Le Coeur de Filet de Boeuf—Sauce Ratafia
*
Les Délices des Belles Forêts aux Herbes
*
Les Pommes de Jersey Rissolés au Four
*
Les Asperges Banchet
Le Beurre Fondu
*
Les Fromages d'Angleterre
Le Céleri Willy
*
La Crêpe sans Souci
Le Rocher Vanille Pittsburgh
*
Le Café
Mignardises

Enclosed in each package is a list of appropriate wines to accompany the meal. To join the BUBBLE-PACK-MEAL-OF-THE-MONTH-CLUB, pick up your phone and dial 1-BUBBLE-PACK.

COOK'S CARDS

START YOUR COLLECTION OF COOK'S CARDS TODAY!

Collect your favorites, such as James Beard, Julia Child, Jacques Pepin, Craig Claiborne and Pierre

A photo of its creator will inspire Real Gourmet cooks to culinary heights when they prepare the recipe on each Cook's Card.

Franey (counts as one card), Piero Scungilli, Paul Bocuse, Ma Tooker, and many others.

A great gift for those Real Gourmet friends, brides, and trivia collectors. ORDER TODAY!

COOK'S CARDS
PO Box 271
Welcome Mat, NY 12256

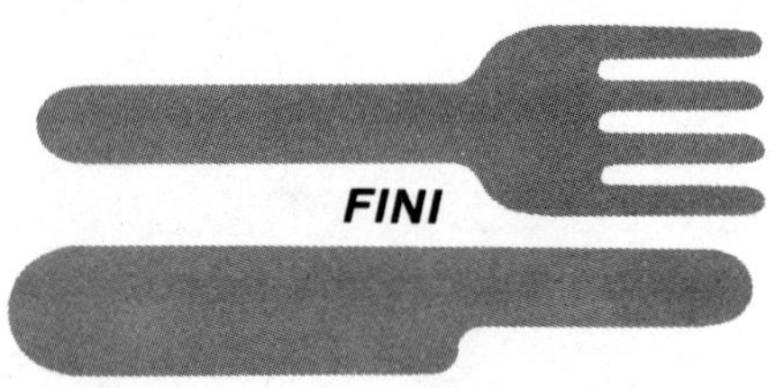